'F'
IS FOR
FLY-FISHING

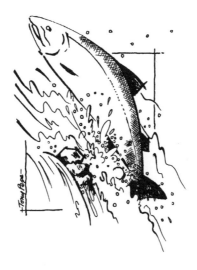

Fiona Armstrong

'F'
IS FOR
FLY-FISHING

Fiona Armstrong

Foreword by Bill Currie

Neil Wilson Publishing • Glasgow

Published by Neil Wilson Publishing Ltd
309, The Pentagon Centre
36 Washington Street
GLASGOW G3 8AZ
Tel: 041-221-1117
Fax: 041-221-5363

The moral right of the author has been asserted.
A catalogue record for this book is available from the British Library.
ISBN 1-897784-09-0

Drawings by Tony Pepe

Typeset in 12.5 on 14pt Palatino by
Face to Face Design Services, Glasgow

Printed in Musselburgh by Scotprint Ltd

Contents

Foreword

*T*he sage who said, 'Every angler was once a beginner, bungling his first casts and fumbling his knots', was guilty of several sins of omission. Firstly he forgot to say that a growing number of new fishers are women; secondly he forgot to go on and say that each beginner is unique. Fiona Armstrong proves these points memorably. Her book is a gem — a fresh, sparkling and individual account by a lively woman of her road into fly-fishing.

'F' Is For Fly-Fishing reminds us all that fishing is not just one world, but a complicated blend of countryside, places and people — not forgetting fish and the tackle we use to catch them. This book takes us all back to our first days with a garden cane, our first trout, our first successes and failures and it catches the spirit of discovery and delight which winds us all into fishing. But it takes us much further, into the developing skills and growing experience of a dedicated and enthusiastic fisher. Enquire within for a story with layer upon layer of interest. It is funny, delightfully anecdotal, sometimes quite serious and often unobtrusively instructional. The light-in-hand style — very immediate and fresh, conceals that its author is in fact really a rather deeply committed and skilful fisher. If this book makes you laugh (and it surely will), it will also teach you much. As in fishing itself, there is a fascinating Chinese box here, with interest within interest, taking you into the delights of the world of fly-fishing.

When I read Fiona's book for the first time, I was delighted to meet several old fishing friends in it — people like Willie Donald of Keswick and Malcolm Greenhalgh among them. I also felt curiously at home with some of the incidents, one or two of which took place on waters I fish regularly. When I finished the book, I realised how skilfully the whole fly-fishing stage had been filled by the author, how well the spirit of the sport had been caught and how good I felt after following Fiona Armstrong down the particular path which led her to the waterside.

It is not surprising that I know of no other fishing book which begins with a swarm of bees coming down the chimney. Nor do I know of any other fishing book which weaves into the text so skillfully such bizarre but memorable waterside incidents. This book is what all good fishing books should be, a sharing of the joy of fishing, which far too many anglers, steeped in the serious business of catching fish, may have begun to ignore.

Bill Currie
(Consultant editor of *Salmon, Trout & Sea-Trout*)
Lilliesleaf,
August 1993

First get your rod

*I*t was one of those mornings. I just knew it. To start with, it was Monday and we'd all overslept. Baby Natasha, normally a cheerfully reliable alarm clock, had for once decided she needed an extra hour and let us down. We'd also just moved house and unable to stand the sight of any more of those cardboard packing-boxes that littered every room, I decided that a change of scenery was the order of the day, so I bundled my daughter into the car and off we drove to the nearby town to shop.

Of course, I have had all the time in the world this summer, for I am now, as my husband describes me, a lady of leisure, having just left a challenging but exhausting job with breakfast TV to spend more time with my family at our home in the Scottish Borders. However, leisure does not preclude the need to shop for unexciting things like washing powder, baked beans and, as I'm discovering, deal with other domestic problems too!

Arriving back a couple of hours later, my mood not improved by the queues at the supermarket check-out, nor the size of my bill, I noticed a man up a telegraph pole at the side of the garden.

'Excuse me, can I ask what you're doing?'

'Oh, it's alright', he said chattily, 'I'm just rigging up a wire across your garden. It'll run over the lawn and meet up with that other post over there.'

I looked nonplussed. 'But I don't want a wire across my garden!'

'Oh, it's alright. In a few months, it'll be like it's always been there!'

'Oh no, it won't! Please come down at once.'

'But I've nearly finished!'

'Look, just stop what you're doing and please, come down!'

So he did, and off I stomped into the house to phone my husband, who's quite good on these sort of things and would, hopefully soon be there to sort everything out. Except that I never made it as far as the phone. As I opened the door, there was a hum, an angry hum as I noticed with horror a hallway full of bees. Now I've been near bees in hives and I've been near bees on flowers and it's never fazed me, but this was something else. Thousands and thousands of bees, all trapped and trying to get out of my house. Some flying frantically round and round, others clustered and hanging like bunches of grapes from the windows. My little daughter was enchanted. 'Buzz, buzz!', she cooed. I quickly shut the door, ran out to my poor man on the lawn, who by now had resignedly taken down his length of wire.

'Listen, are you any good with bees?' I gasped. 'The house is full of them!'

'Sorry,' he said, and added, 'but I had noticed them swarming earlier near your chimney and then going down it.' Thanks a million, I thought.

Well, such things happen when you live in the country and I really wouldn't live anywhere else, but at this particular moment, the stress of a chaotic newsroom and the heart-stopping countdown to a live television show seemed rather more appealing than the strains of rural living.

There was only one thing to do. The bees could wait until my husband, a seasoned beekeeper, arrived home. The man up the pole had by now gone. I took baby to granny, collected my rod and reel and went fishing. It was the only way to unwind from it all and I went down to the water with a growing sense of excitement at the thought of landing a sea-trout or an even an early salmon.

The largest fish I've ever been close to, however, wasn't a salmon, but a Niger perch, which arrived outside our African compound, spread-eagled across a rusty, old bicycle, with head and tail trailing dolefully on the ground. Its owner was the local bush 'fishmonger' and our cook, Johnstone — with a curry, always a curry, in mind — carefully chose a small portion from this 40-pound monster of the deep. It just happened to be the centre steaks. Poor chap! The puzzled look on his face as he tried to balance the two remaining ungainly halves on his bicycle is one of my endearing childhood memories!

Others include playing in the shade of the mango trees, trying to hide from the unforgiving Nigerian sun. Barefoot and brown, we became experts at making the most of what the bush had to offer. To my disgust and against my mother's express wishes, my two brothers, Kit and Patrick, would lift hot, sandy stones to unmask a small snake or a scorpion or some other unsavoury creepy-crawly. As befits a girl, I was rather more ladylike and could usually be seen, net in hand, chasing the huge, birdlike butterflies that flitted in and out of the beautiful frangipani bushes. Now, older and hopefully wiser, it seems a crime to trap such entrancing creatures, but then a friend of my parents, an avid collector, had rather rashly offered to pay sixpence for each multicoloured offering and in those days sixpence went a long way, especially in Africa. My fortune was not to be made, however, as our friend soon reneged on the deal when I started turning up with dozens of specimens and expecting payment!

As teenagers we returned home to Lancashire, where I made up for all those isolated years, wearing the latest fashions and learning the latest dances. With school exams behind me, I travelled south to study at London University, throwing myself wholeheartedly into the round of clubs and pubs that make up a capital city. I whirled from university to local radio, from radio to television. London to Manchester via Reading; more cities, more nightlife, more newsrooms. As a journalist, I reported on all manner of subjects, like the emerging 'green' scene, travelling with Greenpeace to monitor alleged pollution off the Irish sea by nuclear and chemical waste, but as a self-confessed townie, there wasn't a green wellie in sight.

School was held in the morning in the shade of the long, cool verandah, over which crimson bougainvillæa trailed. There, before the sun got up, my brothers and I would sit at tiny desks working away under the watchful eye of my mother. When the heat became too fierce, it was siesta time, but after that, as the sun dipped and the sky softened, we were let loose, free to climb trees and find new, childish treasures, as long as we didn't stray too far. Safaris, on which family and cook would squeeze into a jeep and set off into the bush were a highlight. To keep us quiet, it wasn't, 'See how many red cars you can count', but 'Spot the lion,' or 'Spot the elephant'. Closer to home, pets comprised Betsy the dog, a baby deer and a hilarious monkey, whose party trick was to tightrope the washing line, rather badly, I might add, for like the washing, he spent most of his time upside down, clinging on like mad and swinging in the wind.

In fact, if I ever thought about fishing, it was probably when some river story landed on my reporter's desk. So my angling knowledge could be summed up thus: fishing was something you were born to. Your father did it, and your grandfather probably did it too. Fishermen, (never women, who'd far more sense) were rather eccentric beings. After leaving the wife at home, they would don oversized, old-fashioned waterproofs and sit out in all weathers, usually sheltering under an umbrella, hurling I know not what into murky pools. Apart from irritating the local fish population, they were also a great danger to wildlife, as according to the literature put out in those days by the anti-brigade, all fishers used poisonous lead weights to trap their unsuspecting prey, which inevitably got lost in the water or on the bank and ended up in the gullet of some poor, innocent swan. And, like the attraction, the equipment was a complete mystery. To me, shooting a line was something one did in clever conversation at a party. Reels were Scottish dances, casting something to do with knitting, flies a nuisance at a picnic.

So what changed? Well, it was going to work in the Borders. Ah, what a glorious job, as a reporter and presenter with the local television station. As the name suggests, Border TV straddles England and Scotland, covering land north and south of Hadrian's Wall. Although it's a relatively small company, it takes in one of the largest areas of all the independent television stations but most of the region is countryside. It is, they say, the land where men are men and animals are nervous and, on first sight, there certainly seemed to be more sheep than viewers around. After a few months, though, I realised what a blessing that was. As an added bonus, this was the area where my father was born. Little did I know, I had finally come home.

With the waters and mountains of the Lake District, and the hills and forests of the Borders to explore, work took on a whole new meaning. Apart from the occasional crime story, or the odd flare-up at Sellafield, the nuclear reprocessing plant, stories were now centred largely on farming and tourism. So I bought the statutory green wellies and started adjusting to a new rural life.

Cutting off from the city was hard at first and not without withdrawal symptoms. I remember my first summer, being sent to film a climber who delighted in conquering sheer cliff faces. Now this fellow had done battle with the best of peaks, but on this occasion, he'd discovered a particular one in the Lake District which was so steep that he'd christened it "Arthur Scargill Crag". In other words, it was certainly no pushover! Well it sounded quite a challenge, but I was prepared with sensible outdoor clothing, the hardy climbing boots, the lot. It was only when we actually reached the foot of this monster hill that it dawned on me that I was still wearing rather an excessive amount of jewellery. Thus came the words, 'Hang on a minute, and I'll just take off my pearls before we climb this mountain!' Scottie the cameraman and the rest of the crew were in hysterics.

Yes, it took some getting used to; to realise that cows won't automatically attack when you cross their field, and that they're probably more scared than you are; to understand why local farmers kill foxes, if not accept the way it's often done; to lie awake at night and hear nothing but complete and utter silence.

For someone more used to being lulled to sleep, first as a child by the haunting noises of the African bush, then later by the hustle and bustle of the city, it was a world full of surprises. But it was a world in which I increasingly wanted to live and when I bought a local paper with the headline, *Man in Court for Causing Criminal Damage to an Ash-tray*, I knew I was right.

A year had passed and I still hadn't given fishing much thought. The irony was, that by this time, I was living in a village on the banks of one of Britain's finest salmon rivers, the Eden. After work, I'd walk by the waterside, marvelling at each new revelation thrown up by the various seasons and there would be men, swathed in green rubber, standing up to their waists or even deeper in the water. By now, I'd realised what they were doing, but that was more or less the extent of my interest. I also knew, because the locals told me, that not just anyone could do it, as they were rather a select band, belonging to a group called the Yorkshire Fly-Fishers. The name meant nothing to me then. Now, though, it's got a magical ring to it, the sort of word that gets an angler's knees trembling with excitement, especially if he's got the chance to fish on any of their water!

Two years on and two wonderful things happened to me. I met my future husband and I started to learn to fish. The first was by chance really. Introduced by a friend, love at first sight, you know the sort of thing. We got married fairly quickly and the rest just followed. He'd been brought up to the country and had been out on the river, rod in hand, since he was a toddler, so there was really no question about me having a go. I'm always thankful that he wasn't into football because, no matter how blind love is, I'd have found it much more difficult working up an enthusiasm on the sidelines! To cut a long story short, he took me to a river and amazingly I caught fish, so the interest grew. Then I met the rest of the family, and they all fished, so that was that. No looking back.

Then I landed a great job at ITN and, reluctantly, back to London I went. But I was determined that a city would never be my world again, and it hasn't been. I've worked in the capital for the last six years, and loved every heart-stopping minute of being at the hot end of the studio lights. But the Borders have always been my home, a place for family and friends and fishing; a place to unwind and to leave the city behind.

I have to admit I catch very few fish and after yet another fruitless, or as we say in the trade, blank day, people ask, 'why on earth do you do it?' Admittedly, it's sometimes hard to explain the attraction. When it's early spring and you're on a fishing holiday in the Highlands and it's day five of standing thigh-high in a freezing river with no sign of a tadpole, still less a fresh-run salmon, then a week in Spain does tend to look inviting. But land that fish and I guarantee that you too will be hooked! That's just why I do it — I am hopelessly hooked on it all; from the delight of solitude and the complete and utter peace of being by the riverside to the companionship of other anglers and the trembling excitement of having a fighting fish on the end of the line; from the exhilaration of winning to, more often than not, the frustration of losing, the fresh air, the exercise. Let me explain more.

Fishing is Britain's most popular participant sport, with more than four million enthusiasts. That's a lot of people, a lot of time and a mountain of money too! Millions of pounds spent annually on tackle, on permits and on angling magazines and books. All of it in pursuit of a fish, but it's all done in different ways.

The sea-angler, as his name suggests, has the choice of fishing from a beach or from a boat, sometimes in exotic locations, catching anything from flounder to blue marlin. Then there's the coarse fisher, which is the name given to the person who sits by rivers and canals to catch fish such as roach and perch. There's hearty competition amongst coarse fishers to see who can land the biggest and best catches of the day. At major events, they draw lots for their position on the bank and stay in that place all day, more often than not under large umbrellas which make a colourful sight along the water's edge. Coarse fishers do not kill their catches. They usually weigh them and return them to the water at the end of the day.

I am what is known as a game fisher, an angler who fishes in rivers, lakes and lochs for salmon, sea-trout or trout, rarely staying in one spot, but moving up, down and across the river and frequently in it! Now, game fishers often kill what they catch and eat it. They can use what's known as a spinning-rod and a spinning-reel, with all manner of bait on the end, from wooden lures to worms, but it's generally accepted that the purest form of game fishing is fly-fishing, which basically involves using a 12 to 15 foot rod and artificial flies dressed on a hook using a mix of feather, hair, silk and tinsel.

Now, a mystique has grown up about who fishes what and where and when, and it's all very silly. For example, it used to be said that coarse fishing was the sport for the working class, a chance for the factory labourer to throw his hook into the canal after a tiring day in the mill. A little further up the scale, with slightly more money to spend, the middle class, the doctors and the lawyers would take to the sea in search of cod and mackerel. While at the top end, there was the upper class, the landowners whose money bought leisure and the chance to fish for salmon.

Well, times change and all for the better, as far as I'm concerned because if those rules still stood, I'd have no chance of becoming a game fisher! Yes, thankfully, these days everything's much more mixed. Although it's true that fly-fishing is often perceived as a purist form of the

With Commander William Donald and the late Michael Cartmell on the
Branski Beat (I kid you not!), River Eden

sport and you do get the odd snobby remark, 'My dear, it's the *only* way to do it...', of course it isn't. There can often be as much skill in fishing upstream with a worm as there is with a fly. But for me, fly-fishing is certainly the most satisfying type of angling and in my short time out and about on rivers north and south, I've met many different people from varying walks of life who fish a fly.

Only the other week, I came into contact with a midwife in London, who told me that her sure way of getting away from babies and pregnant mums was to head up to the Highlands to fish the River Oykel with a fly-rod. I've met butchers, I've met bakers, (good friends, Michael Cartmell — now sadly deceased, and John Bryson, both from Keswick); I've yet to meet a candlestick maker, but I'm sure there is one out there who also loves the lure of the feathered hook.

It's a shame that fly-fishing for salmon is perceived as an elitist sport, since it certainly doesn't have to be. But I suppose the misconceptions are understandable. I've just been filmed for a Channel Four programme, appropriately called Screaming Reels, which promises to be a cracker of a show and the presenter, Nick Fisher, a wonderfully knowledgeable and keen angler, confessed to me that he'd been an angler since he was a boy, but he had never really considered game fishing because in his words, he felt he wasn't *allowed* to fish for salmon. That's a refreshingly honest opinion and I can understand that view, but, let me assure you, you are allowed!

You don't need to have pots of money and you don't have to have a title — mind you, I'm not saying that it wouldn't help, but then you could say that about anything. Age is no bar either, and the younger you start fishing the better. Our young friend Jamie Hammond caught his first salmon, a most respectable 10 pounder, at the tender age of eight and as he relates it, he struggled with this unwieldy rod for what seemed like a lifetime, before he valiantly brought it to the net. What a game wee fellow he was, for I remember his fish well and it was almost as large as he was.

Jamie Hammond, aged eight with his first salmon! He caught it on a spinning rod, but now fishes a fly

Neither is sex a handicap, and although we lady anglers are outnumbered ten-to-one by the men, we can still give them a run for their money . Several of my girlfriends regularly outfish their menfolk, including my mother-in-law, Pat (who never returns from a fishing trip without at least one salmon) and our pal Viv Clough, a Carlisle lawyer, who frequently arrives at our house with a boot full of fish and a huge smile on her face. This year, she says she's been too busy to go down to the river more than once or twice, so the salmon in the river Eden are safe for the moment!

The record books also prove it. The biggest salmon caught on rod and line in British waters was landed by a woman, Miss Georgina Ballantine. It was on the Tay in the 1920s and the fish weighed a staggering 64 pounds. Two years later, Mrs Clementina Morrison broke the record for a salmon caught on the fly; 61 pounds on the Deveron. Why we females seem to catch large fish is a matter of some debate, but the latest theory, (put forward by a man, no doubt!) is that it's less to do with our angling ability, and rather more to do with our pheromones; the suggestion being that the fish are in some way attracted by female hormones. I really don't know about that. I just agree with the person who pointed out that if it were the men who caught all the big fish, no-one would dream of looking for a reason why!

I've fished a spinning-rod; sometimes, when the river's so high, there's nothing else to do. I've also fished a worm. 'Poaching with a garden fly', my husband jokingly calls it, but the most satisfying thing for me is the click, swish of the fly-rod as it shoots the lure across the water. The feel of the line in your fingers as it turns round in the current, the hope, and then sometimes, just sometimes mind, the bite as the rod-tip judders with the take!

Every angler will tell you a different story about the attraction of fly-fishing for salmon. I like the one from our chimney sweep. 'It doesn't matter if you don't catch anything, it's the anticipation. You feel it here,' he said, touching his breast. 'Sometimes they take, sometimes they don't; but you feel it, every bit of it, the nibbles, the flutters, the pulls. Fishing for salmon is the most exciting thing of all!'

More exciting than putting out a live broadcast? True there are faint similarities between the two. The preparation for both is, hopefully, methodical and carefully researched. The studio is lit, the microphones and cameras checked, as are the news facts. In the same way, the rod is assembled, the correct lure attached, the weather conditions and the position of the fish ascertained. The cast out into the river is measured and calm, just as the delivery of a good bulletin should be. In both cases, when the action starts there's the inward excitement as the adrenaline flows, but the outward calm as you strive to stay in control.

Newscasting and fly-casting. Both are unpredictable and both can be fraught with danger. Will that late story which broke just as you went on air ever arrive? Why did the film that you confidently introduced, (three times) never materialise? And why, in all the chaos of an early-morning breakfast show, did you have someone sitting next to you, when you hadn't a clue who they were? So that when the director called out, 'Ten seconds to On-Air!', you panicked and turned in desperation to ask this strange lady which interview she was in for. I shall never forget the answer — a rather puzzled 'I really don't know'. She was in fact somebody's relative who'd just wandered by accident onto the set and sat herself down on our big, comfy sofa!

In just the same way, when you're by the river, you know that elusive fish is there somewhere, but will he make an appearance? You've done everything right, but is he going to take your lure; and, if he does, will the line hold and the hook stay firm? Up he goes, jumping out of

First get your Rod...fishing on the River Tay

the water! A nerve-racking moment. Now, how can you possibly get him into the bank without losing him? Just like a live programme, in fishing there's generally only one go at it so there's no room for error.

You might now be asking. 'She's only been fishing for six years. What does she know about it?' Answer, not a lot. So what on earth am I doing writing a book about the subject? Well, it occurred to me that not knowing a great deal, but having learnt a little through a great many mistakes, I might just be the right person to pass on a few beginner's tips and a few humorous tales. Some starting points for those who might not quite be ready for the weightier words of famed fishers far superior to me. Thus, a great deal of this is written on instinct and early experience. I've been extremely fortunate to have had the help and advice of Neil Graesser OBE, fishing author and salmon expert. He recognised that there may be a niche for such a book. 'Go for it', he said. I hope you do, too. I've also picked the very knowledgeable brains of Crawford Little and Malcolm Greenhalgh. Bill Currie has also been kind enough to write a foreword too. Thank you to them and to all my friends and family who kept me well supplied with stories, some more apocryphal than others.

Then there's my husband, without whom a line would not have been cast or written, a fly tied or a wonderful new world opened up. Oh, and by the way, his name is Rod.

Learning to fish

Angling may be said to be so like the mathematics, that it can never be fully learnt.

Isaak Walton, *The Compleat Angler, 1653*

I've always been hopeless at maths, but at the age of 16, I scraped through my 'O' level with a rotten grade and how I rejoiced! Never again would I have to bend my simply non-mathematical mind round an utterly incomprehensible page of algebra or fractions. I definitely think that I've a good chance of getting a better grade in fishing. It's not that it's *that* easy, for angling can be hard work and at times it is unpredictable and infuriating, but at least it's fun and I promise that the resulting satisfaction and enjoyment is well worth the effort.

As a beginner, you will probably need to persevere for quite a while because, like most jobs, television presenting included, there's only one way to become proficient and that's to do it, time and time again. Theory is all very well, but no matter how many practise runs you do, be it broadcasts or fly-casts, nothing prepares you for the excitement and terror of that first live report as you count down to takeoff and the red light goes on, or that first, fearful cast with a long, long salmon rod.

So how do you learn to fish? If you're now sitting in an office in the middle of a city, reading this and thinking — yes, I'd like to fish for salmon but I don't know any fishers and I haven't got a clue how to go about it — what can you do? Basically, you've got to try and meet some other fishers; once you've done that, they'll hopefully introduce you to a veritable network of other anglers. Some of you may already have friends who are fishers, so let them know that you're interested in taking up the sport and ask them if you can come along on a trip which would be suitable for a beginner.

If you don't know any fishers, (and why should you, as I certainly didn't six years ago) what you should do is to look through the adverts of established angling magazines and find a good fly-fishing course. If the teacher is a member of the Association of Professional Game Angling Instructors (APGAI) then you'll be taught by the best. After an introductory tuition course, there should be no looking back but you will know in your own mind whether the sport is for you or not.

I must say, I didn't undertake any early professional lessons, but I wish I had, because it's rather like driving a car or learning to swing a golf club. Learning the correct way from the start means you probably won't pick up too many bad habits and that's quite important in angling. So get hold of that magazine and find out about a course, which should include tuition with an expert angler, plus the chance to practice on a salmon river. Lessons however aren't cheap and a day can cost £100 or more, depending on who the teacher is. If it's somebody famous, you'll obviously pay extra, but in a case like this it may be that fewer hours are needed, so you've got to decide how much time and money you can afford. The personal touch, with one-to-one tuition, is obviously best, but I'm told that learning with a group can be great fun, especially where overnight accommodation is included.

I'll try to tell you more about the technicalities of fly-fishing later in the book; suffice to say here, that casting that lure out into the water is an art in itself and every teacher has his or her own way of demonstrating it. Some prefer to start well away from the water, with no trees, bushes or banks to get in the way, so they may show the basic moves on a lawn or in an open field. Others throw the beginner in at the deep end and make straight for the river where, who knows, you may instantly catch a fish and be hooked. Such is life with some beginners simply

All washed out on the Oykel after a flood. No fishing today...

luckier than others. And some are better off than others too, so if a beginner can't afford to hire a professional tutor, he must do the next best thing and persuade a friend or relation to teach him. A word of caution here; although this is a relatively inexpensive way to learn about fishing, (your only outgoings being bribes and presents) it's not necessarily an easy way, so choose your tutor carefully!

Though I love him dearly, it's fair to say that my husband and I had some slight disagreements in my early angling days. In fact when I think of it, getting your better half to teach you to fish is a minefield, worse than a husband teaching a wife to drive. It's not that Rod's a bad tutor, because I've heard him with other beginners and he is, quite frankly, excellent. He's patient, informative and fun, but when we first fished together it was a different matter altogether. Maybe it's just that we were too close and he wanted so badly for me to get it right and I wanted so badly to do it right! Whatever the reason, I found that as a complete beginner it was much easier to learn the basics from someone else.

The thing is that watching as a beginner, it all looks so easy. Just throw back the line, cast away and Bob's your uncle! Or is he? Because it's only when you actually hold that frightening and clumsy salmon-rod in trembling fingers that the truth about timing and handling begins to dawn. In fact, looking back on it now, teaching the novice to fish must be a nightmare. For a start, the instructor runs the certain risk of being scarred for life after being hit by flailing line and fly. And even if he's got nerves of steel, unless he's also got bags of patience, he's likely to get pretty fed-up with repeating what seem to him to be perfectly simple instructions, like, 'Up, back, pause, forward, and let go!' The line that is, not the whole rod and reel to. Ah, well! On the other hand, the long-suffering teacher may get a real know-all...

It was 1986, my first attempt at fishing, and Rod and I had travelled up to Aberdeenshire to fish one of Scotland's finest salmon rivers, the mighty Dee. Experienced fishers reading this will no doubt be most impressed, not to say outraged, at the waste of such a wonderful water on a mere beginner. And it was a waste too. Six years on, I appreciate the fact that devotees are prepared to pay hundreds of pounds a week to cast from its hallowed banks, but in those early days, I'm afraid I didn't know the difference between a good water and a dead pool. However, arriving in good time for lunch and settling ourselves into a comfortable fishing hotel at Banchory, we eventually made our way down to the river, rods at the ready, fingers itching to go. It was early spring and we'd only known each other a couple of months, so love was young, with the desire to please on both sides.

'Don't worry, I'll start you off with a spinning-rod', soothed my anxious fiancé. 'It's much easier than fly-fishing, and once you've mastered that, we can make some progress.' Well, it sounded nice and simple, but on rivers like this, you can only use a spinning-rod when the water reaches a certain height and by the time we got down there, we were told, 'Sorry, it's fly-fishing only!'

'Never mind,' said Rod, 'We've got the small fly-rod in the back of the car. A few lessons on the river bank, and we'll soon have it cracked.' How right he was. Cracked on the ear, cracked on the nose, cracked on the back of the head. Even though the first few casts were flyless, 25 metres of plastic-coated line can still deliver a hefty whack to whichever bit of the anatomy is unfortunate enough to be in the way! Half-an-hour into the proceedings and my loved one's patience was wearing thin. 'Fiona, don't throw it, flick it. I've told you, let the rod do the work!'

'I'm *not* throwing it...'

'You are...look for God's sake, just watch where you're putting that thing!'

'Now don't tell me to watch where I put it. I *know* what I'm doing, and it's not me, it's the rod that's putting itself there!'

'Oh have it your own way! I'll put on a fly for you, and you can practice by yourself. I'm going down-river to do some fishing myself.'

And off he went. And there I was with a 12 foot 6 inch salmon-rod in my hands — small by fly-fishing standards — but still enormous to a novice and an increasing desperation to get this wildly flailing line and lure under control. An hour later and the fly was well and truly living up its name. Flying up trees, banks and my nose. And then, it actually landed where it was supposed to. On the water. My first half-reasonable cast and bang! 'Help!' I yelled, as the reel jerked into life, 'There's something on the end. What do I do?!' Of course there was no answer, my loved one having taken himself to a position of safety, as far down the river as possible. So, realising that no-one was going to come, but remembering vaguely what I'd been told to do, I started to wind and wind, until there was nothing left to wind. When Rod eventually put in an appearance, there I was, standing on the bank, rod held high with a small, sorry-looking sea-trout swinging from the end. Hardly the conventional way to land your quarry! Needless to say, the man I planned to marry was immensely impressed, not to say stunned. First came a big kiss and hug, and then came a lecture on the rights and wrongs of it all. 'Supposing it had been a salmon you'd hooked; winding the fish up to the rod-point would have broken it.'

Well, to cut a long story short, I duly took his advice, and the next couple of sea-trout I caught were brought gently and rather more conventionally to the bank. It was rather funny really since, throughout all this performance, there was another chap fishing from the opposite bank who had been looking rather amused at my pathetic attempts to flog the water, as he fished away with great aplomb. The grin faded from his face when I got the first catch and by the time I'd laid my third fish on the bank, he couldn't contain himself any longer. 'I say, what sort of flies are you using?', he shouted over.

'Oh, just a Hairy Mary', I replied nonchalantly, though I hadn't a clue. I'd heard that name bandied about by other anglers and this fly was red and black and quite hairy too, so it could have been a Mary. My fellow fisher was last seen searching through his tackle bag to see if he had one. Incidentally, if another angler starts to catch fish, you will want to know what sort of fly he's using too. I know that I've been on rivers where no-one is touching anything and then suddenly someone gets a bite on a two-inch tube-fly and presto! everyone rushes back to their car to find their two-inch tube-flies. Of course, it usually doesn't work and still no-one touches anything, but we all think we're in with a chance and that's vitally important when fishing.

Catching something on my first outing was no doubt beginner's luck. If there is such a thing, of course, for you'll find that everyone has their own little theory about why a newcomer to the sport can initially be so successful. The one I like best of all is that whereas the experienced fisher is generally a consistent and smooth caster, the novice is unpredictable. With erratic movements, his line is usually going here, there and everywhere and it's this jerkiness which either tantalises the

A 10lb fresh run spring salmon, caught on the Oykel

fish or irritates him into snapping at the fly. Another view is that the beginner catches more fish because he's doing things more slowly and methodically, or he may be wading slowly and therefore covering the water more thoroughly. Whatever the theory, it seems that as a newcomer, you definitely have a sporting chance of coming up trumps, so get cracking!

*Mike Bullough,
his luckless wife
Sandy and Rod*

There are exceptions to the rule though and, despite their best efforts, some folk never catch anything and this is awful as there's nothing worse than repeated failure. Obviously if you're consistently drawing a blank, you become despondent. Take my friend Sandy Bullough. Now, her husband Mike is a dedicated and excellent angler, who regularly invites us to fish the River Tay near Perth. He's the ace fly-fisher and Sandy is the fisher's dream partner, a real trooper who puts up with all his mad angling friends with their wet wellies and their endless, tall stories of outsized salmon. She generously and happily provides picnics and a sympathetic ear, but although she throws herself wholeheartedly into the angling scene, these days she's not actually that keen on rushing down to the river and casting a line herself. And it's not that she throws a bad one. On the contrary, she's more polished than I am for she knows what she's doing and she knows how to do it properly. But the thing is, Sandy has fished for 17 years and in all that time, she's never caught anything!

Oh, she's been near to it once or twice. Like the time she flogged away for hours in the wind, the cold and the rain, casting stoically, until her wrists ached and her fingers froze. Then finally, in desperation, she asked the ghillie to take the rod for a few minutes while she returned to the car to fetch a pair of dry gloves. Yes, you've guessed it, just as she left the bank, there was a splash and a gasp, as the ghillie hooked a salmon. Not just any old fish, mind you, for this was a prize 27-pounder. Oh, there was some excitement to the event, as the ghillie gave her the rod and she was able to land the thing and I suppose she could have claimed it, but she didn't, because she didn't actually hook it. So now, all these blank years on, she's convinced, not only does she not catch fish, she actually prevents others from doing so. 'I'm afraid I'm a Jonah', she says. Well, I used to pay no attention to that, but I must admit, empty hours spent on river banks do fuel the fires of superstition and it's true, every time Sandy is near, no-one catches anything!

But she's not alone, for there's the poor fellow I met on the River Dee last year. He'd been going there for 18 years, taking a week's fishing each year, the highlight of his angling calendar, in fact the only fishing he ever did, but he floored me when he said that in all that time, he'd never caught a salmon either. Now that's either dedication, madness or worse.

So much for beginner's luck! But whenever and however you land your first salmon, it promises to be a day to remember. For whatever it looks like, and whatever it tastes like, it will be your first and you'll dine out on the story for years to come; like I do with mine.

It was 1988, my second year of fishing, and our first wedding anniversary and after a few days touring in central Scotland, including a trip on a steam train and an entertaining few hours trying to spot the Loch Ness monster, we decided to head further north. I'd always wanted to go to the very top of the United Kingdom, so we thought we'd try for John O'Groats. Well, we've never been there yet, as lured by the thought of a few Highland salmon, we stopped off en route at a lovely fishing hotel in Sutherland where Rod's parents had been taking a short break. Of course, that was it and what started as a cup of tea and ten minutes by the water ended in a four day stay, though I was never to regret it. It was the Achness Hotel on the River Cassley, and it's what I call a real fishing hotel, warm and welcoming, with mountains of hearty Scottish food, a bar full of ghillies and salmon tales, and a guest list that consists almost exclusively of other mad-keen anglers.

The first day was spent enjoyably watching, especially when my father-in-law Tommy caught a salmon and I was able to net it for him, and rather nicely too I thought, though it was done with trembling hands and a fluttering heart. It's a great responsibility landing someone else's fish! The next day, though, it was his turn to return the favour.

It was just after lunch and we went down to the House pool on the lower part of the river. I'd already been out by the water for most of the morning and was beginning to despair. Would my casting ever improve? 'Come on, I'll give you some lessons', said Tommy and I was grateful, for he's a man who's fished all his life and is an excellent teacher, someone who's calm and who doesn't panic or get exasperated if you're less than quick in putting theory into practice. In fact, going back to our driving theme, he's like the good instructor, who instead of becoming hysterical when his pupil shows no sign of stopping at a red light, calmly suggests that he might touch the brake ever so slightly.

And there we were, the two of us. He trying to explain the finer points of casting, me trying to learn from his many years of wisdom and experience. 'Plop!' Another failure as the line ended miserably in a loop in front of us. He said nothing, but out of the corner of my eye, I could see him trying to keep a straight face as my cast bit the dust, or in this case, the water. Then, the next one was half — well maybe just a quarter — decent. 'I've got a fish!', I gasped, 'and it's a big one!' and in the excitement, I jerked the rod up.

'Careful now, careful!', he cautioned, but too late! With a mixture of over-enthusiasm and panic, I yanked up the rod and the poor old fish came flying out of the water and onto the side of the bank. 'Oh no!' shouted Tommy, the calm exterior crumbling as he desperately tried to think of something to do to stop the whole thing ending in disaster. It didn't, you'll be relieved to hear. My salmon fell back into the river, but I somehow managed to tighten the line and get matters under control.

'It looks a bit red', said Tommy, 'We may have to put it back.'

'No!', I shouted rather unsportingly. 'It's not going back!' I wouldn't have cared if it was blue with purple spots. I just knew that it was a salmon and it was mine. And you'll find that too. When you catch your first salmon, it might be the oldest, blackest, most rotten fish in the river, but to you, it will seem like an oil painting. And it was beautiful too because some ten frantic minutes later, we were examining a nine pound fish. My first salmon!

Well, I like to think I've done some exciting and heart-stopping things in my life, most of them to do with my job as an on-the-road reporter. I've been in racing cars and helicopters, been driven at over 100mph by a blind driver, paraglided over the Aegean sea and I've looked down the barrel of a African gun after being stopped by troops in the Ugandan bush But my first salmon! It must surely rank among the ones to remember. Oh, I nearly sang for joy and was only sorry that there hadn't been more people around to witness this great event, though, looking back now, I suppose I should have been grateful that we were relatively unobserved. It was hardly the most graceful catch, even for a beginner!

Now you may think I'm being melodramatic, but really, your first salmon is something you will always remember. The amazement and the panic as you get that initial pull, the fluttering heart and the trembling fingers as you try to bring the fish under control. The interminable wait as you impatiently call for the net to be brought. 'Hurry up, hurry up! Oh, please net it quickly before it has time to get off the hook!'

Advice from fishing expert Neil Graesser OBE, on the River Cassley

And then, the careful landing as the net is raised out of the water and placed on the grass and the incredulous look as it slowly dawns that you have caught your first salmon!

Well, of course, there was great rejoicing in the bar that night, as the tale was told and retold, and the fish got bigger and better each time, all the while being toasted with numerous drams. It was further marked down in history when I bought a map of the river with the successful pool marked clearly in ink. I've since had it framed and mounted on the wall, which means that in depressingly blank months, I can look back and recall glory days. I also keep a fishing diary and would recommend that you do too. Again, when the only thing you're catching on fishing trips is a cold, it's something to keep up the spirits.

Yes, you never forget your first salmon, nor the water you catch it on and to this day, I've always had a soft spot for the Cassley, which incidentally is where I met Neil Graesser, who owns the fishing there. Neil has given lessons to hundreds of would-be anglers and his theory is that you must not baffle the beginner with too much science. Quite right too; what he needs to know are a few basic moves. Then, hopefully, the teacher will stand well back and let him get on with it. As long as he's doing those two things right, other mistakes can wait to be corrected.

In fly-fishing, it's really a case of slowly but surely wins the race. That's the expert advice. Mine, as a novice with a smattering of experience, is to tell you to listen carefully to every word your teacher says. When you're not fishing yourself, sit down in a place well out of harm's way and simply watch. It's surprising just how much can be learned from 30 yards away! Finally, take a note out of a nosey journalist's book and don't be frightened to ask questions about 'why, how, what, where or when', no matter how simple they might seem. You want to get it right, so you may as well start as you mean to go on. So, to take a leaf out of Mrs Beeton's cookery book...'First catch your salmon'!

Where and when to fish

*I went on this expensive fishing holiday and I only caught one fish,
so if you work it out, this salmon has cost me five-hundred pounds!
(Fisher to mother)*

*Well, if it cost you that for one fish, it's a good thing you didn't
catch two! (Mother to fisher)*

W hen I first started working in radio, I remember being told on my
journalism course that, as a reporter, I was entering one of the most
exclusive clubs in the world. That NUJ card, we were informed by our
tutor, was a passport which could take us, young and eager as we were,
freely all over the world. Fifteen years on, I see that he was generally
right, for in my time on the road, I've been lucky enough to cover stories in Britain and Europe and further afield. On the one side, it's been
a ticket to talk to Prime Ministers and Royals. On the other, it's been an
introduction into somebody's home, a chance to meet an ordinary person with a remarkable or heart-rending story to tell. What it hasn't been,
however, is a licence to charge onto somebody's land without permission and, unfortunately, it hasn't been a licence to fish for salmon. As a
newcomer to the angling world, I was under the delusion that if I wanted
to catch a fish, all I had to do was to find a bit of water and get cracking.
Water belongs to everybody, doesn't it? And if it doesn't, there are those
who'd argue that maybe it should do. Well, I was wrong. Like everything else in life, angling has its rules and regulations and you ignore
them at your cost!

So let's establish a few facts. Basically, all fishing for salmon in the
UK is privately owned and although there are different types of owner-
ship, depending on which country you're in, that stretch of salmon water
will belong to someone, either to an individual, a fishing association, a
local authority or to the Crown.

Salmon can be fished for from rivers, river estuaries and lochs, either from the bank, from a small boat or by wading, but wherever the
angler wants to cast a line, he'll need to get permission and usually

have to pay. Whoever owns the water can be put to a deal of expense, because they are liable to look after it, maintaining spawning grounds and repairing and improving pools and banks. In short, the owner's job is to try to make life as comfortable and rewarding as possible for you, the paying fisher.

And just as you can't fish where you want, you can't fish when you want. There's a season and it varies from river to river, but it generally lasts eight to nine months, say from early spring to late autumn. The remaining time, known as the close season, is to cover the spawning period when the salmon lay their eggs and multiply. In England and Wales anglers can fish for salmon every day of the week during the season, but in Scotland, fishing for salmon isn't allowed on a Sunday. I'm told this rule was originally something to do with the Kirk, a law introduced by ministers stop the parishioners by doing anything remotely pleasurable on their one day off!

Fishing out of season, without permission, or with illegal methods, is called poaching and in the old days it was punishable by the chopping-off of hands. Today, retribution is less severe, but fines of £100 and more and the confiscation of expensive tackle, including in some cases, your car, are painful on the pocket. It's also extremely embarrassing to be frogmarched off the river by an irate water bailiff after being caught red-handed in the wrong place. I relate a story told to me by my husband. The names could have been changed to protect the guilty, but never mind. To spare too many blushes, though, I have to say that all this happened a long time ago!

There were two of them, Rod and his best mate Joe. And at a loose end one summer's evening, they decided to pop down to their local village pub for a swift half. 'Just one mind!' Well, you know what it's like. A half became a pint which then headed towards a gallon and before they knew it, it was 11pm and closing time. However it was a beautiful, still night and quite bright too, so the obvious thing to do, in this relaxed state of inebriation, was to go fishing!

It seemed an excellent idea and by midnight our boys had clumsily gathered together their fishing gear and had stumbled down to the river. Any old bit of river, as it happened, because by this time, they'd convinced themselves that as they lived locally, they were well and truly entitled to fish locally! So with headlights blazing to see what they were doing, though they hardly knew what they were doing, they got out rods and reels and got to work.

Joe was the first in the water and as he cast a rather unsteady line he heard voices from the opposite bank. 'Go away!', he shouted boldly. 'This is our river!' Unfortunately, that's not what the water bailiff thought, as he quickly nipped round with his men to find his challenger up to his thighs in water, with one wader fixed and the other tumbling round his ankle. A sodden young man was marched unceremoniously out of the river. His partner in crime meanwhile was some way downstream, trying to disentangle his line from an extremely awkward prickly gorse bush, but on hearing the commotion, he abandoned rod and reel and tried desperately to hide his six-foot frame in amongst the undergrowth. Scratched and bleeding from the unforgiving gorse, he held his breath and waited, but when the water officials started to beat the bushes with huge sticks my husband decided it was time to brazen it out, for the best means of defence, he had heard, can often be attack. 'Good evening, gentlemen. What a lovely evening for a walk!' he said as he stood up. 'Can I ask you what you're doing on this private water?'

'Private water. It certainly *is* private water! And it doesn't belong to you! You're not out for a walk, you're with this other man!'

'I've never seen him before!', said Rod, vowing to make it up to Joe at some later stage.

'Fish, what fish!'

'Thanks mate!' said Joe, indignantly, by now very damp and quite sober and understandably unwilling to take the full rap. To cut a long story short, the sorry pair were marched off the river. Their names and addresses were taken and their equipment was confiscated. It could have been worse though. They could have been taken to court or, had it been a century earlier, they might have been transported to Australia. 'And if I had my way, you buggers would still go!' shouted an irate water bailiff.

I suppose, to be honest, every angler has at some stage fished where he shouldn't, though he'd never dream of calling himself a poacher. Usually, it's totally innocent, like the time I looked across a wonderful stretch of Highland water to see a furious fellow waving his hands about and bellowing, 'What the hell do you think you're doing here?!' I was in fact casting my way quite happily up river. Too happily as it turned out, as in my blinkered enthusiasm I'd wandered well out of my allotted patch and well into foreign territory. You see, it's one thing if you flog the water and disturb the fish if it's your water, but it's quite another if you're making waves on someone else's patch. In this particular case, profuse apologies were grudgingly accepted, for as long as it's a one-off and a genuine mistake, most people will forgive these minor lapses. It's when you look at the extent of serious poaching, you can understand why there's so much concern.

Gone are the times when the locals fished one for the pot-poaching is now big business and a problem which affects not just water owners, but ultimately all anglers. It's impossible to tell exactly how many salmon are taken illegally each year, but it's reckoned to be a significant proportion of stocks. Some are simply netted out in the dead of night, but there are other, more ruthless ways. We once arrived to fish a river in Aberdeenshire to find that a highly-organised gang had been down in the wee small hours and beaten us to it. What they'd done was to use a substance (usually a bag of cement) which removes the oxygen from the water and working in the half-light, in a few minutes they'd managed to clear a whole pool as the asphyxiated salmon floated to the surface and were simply scooped out. That, however, was only the start of the problem because the poison they used not only killed the fish but also wiped everything else out in the pool, with the water left dead for weeks to come.

And just as poachers are ruthless in their methods of killing fish, they can be equally merciless with anyone who gets in their way. One solitary watchman is little match for a determined gang and the water watcher's job can be a dangerous and lonely one, especially at night. It can also be an impossible one, trying to patrol a stretch of river several miles long, so it's not surprising that owners and authorities get twitchy about who's fishing where and when.

So who looks after what? Well, rivers in England and Wales are monitored by a body called the National Rivers Authority. The NRA or 'Guardians of the Water', as they're known, employ bailiffs and water watchers to keep an eye on who's fishing where and catching what and they also give out licences and check on pollution. In Scotland, waters are protected by either the District Fisheries Boards, by local angling associations or by private owners.

Some waters are completely off-bounds, even to genuine anglers. For example, certain spawning grounds may not be fished. I recall that when my husband and I were first house-hunting in the Borders, we came across our dream home, with a small river running by the side! Alas, before we could get too excited, we discovered it was a special spawning-ground and therefore couldn't be touched. We didn't buy the house, needless to say, but had there been a rod available, it would have made the dry rot and the nailsick roof seem much more acceptable!

To sum up. If you cast a line for salmon in any part of the UK, you'll need to get permission, either verbally, or in the form of a written permit, either a day permit, a week permit or whatever. I've found it's a good thing to keep your permit handy when you're fishing because if the water watcher comes along, he may ask to see it and unless he knows you personally, he's unlikely to be impressed by faces, famous or not. Even being a relatively well-known TV presenter doesn't help when it comes to explaining yourself to the water watcher and I speak from experience. 'Oh I know who you are', he said to me as I fumbled about in my tackle-bag for my identification, 'you're that Angela Rippon.'

'Well, actually, no...'

'Oh, you can't fool me, I know you're Angela Rippon! Well I still need to see your card!'

On top of a permit, anyone who fishes for salmon in England or Wales, (though not in Scotland) will also need to buy a rod-licence, and these are obtained from the National Rivers Authority, from local tackle shops or sub-post offices. At one time there used to be all manner of licences, depending on where you were fishing and what you were fishing for, but a recent introduction is the single national rod-licence which covers all kinds of angling, from pike to perch and trout to salmon. It costs £13.25 for the year, which isn't at all bad if you're a regular fisher. Long may it continue, because as a beginner, you're going to need all the bargains going, because salmon fishing is in great demand and can be expensive.

A blissful afternoon on the Border Esk. MIKE SCOTT, SUNDAY SUN

Fishing is a family affair...with my father-in-law, Tommy. Below left: Rod with a beautiful salmon caught on the Dee; and below right: Tommy and Pat with fine catches at the Dee Head beat

Let me expand on this. Most rivers are divided into stretches of water called beats and these are either fished privately or are rented or let to anglers who are often known as tenants. Now a big, world-famous river like the Scottish Dee which is more than 80 miles long, may have up to 50 separate beats, whereas in contrast, a small, unknown spate river may just have one or two beats to its name. A beat can be let for a day, a week, or even longer and it comes either as double or single-bank fishing, that is, it can be fished either from both banks or from just one.

As a beginner however, don't even consider renting until you find your feet, or in this case, your waders. What the trainee fisher should be doing in the early days is cultivating friends, (or even enemies when it comes to fishing) and these should preferably be very rich and also very busy because it means they'll have lots of fishing booked, but very little time to do anything about it, so they'll need some help to make sure it's not wasted! We've had some great invitations to fish some wonderful waters.

What happens is that someone you know might take a week on a particular beat where he's allowed to fish two rods. Now, unless he's Superman, he can't physically fish more than one rod at any one time, so he may invite you to come along to fish the other. As a beginner you may take unashamed advantage of any offer like this, in fact you must positively jump at the chance, but as time goes by and you're no longer seen as the newcomer, you'll need to return favour for favour and heartfelt thanks will simply not be enough. Bottles of malt whisky certainly go some way to showing appreciation and these are usually swiftly and gratefully pounced on by any angler worth his salt, but if you regularly accept fishing from someone, sooner or later you'll be expected to reciprocate and that will mean buying or renting some of your own.

So what's available? Well, if money's no problem, you could go the whole hog and consider the small estate. You know the idea, the big house with a couple of hundred acres and a small salmon river running through the middle. A few million should do the job there. See *Country Life, The Field* and other upmarket magazines for details!

If, however, that's a little optimistic, the next step down could be a fishing timeshare. Now, this is where you buy a day or a week per year on a specific river for the next 30 years or so, or even for life. It's still expensive, (costing thousands rather than millions) but the theory is that, over the years, like a fine painting, it'll prove to be a good investment. There are drawbacks, though. Firstly, do you really want to have the same beat at the same time for the next 30 years? For unless it can be sublet or a swop can be organised with another angler, that's what's involved. Also, it's very difficult to predict how waters will fare in the future and places that fish well in the 1990s might well prove disappointing in the 21st century, a fact borne out many times when a hitherto excellent salmon river suddenly takes a dramatic dive in fortunes as stocks dwindle or as pools silt up when the river changes course. On the other hand, though, if your bright star is shining, it might well improve!

And that brings us on to how rivers are valued. Beats are generally priced according to the number of salmon caught there. Take our River Dee again; expensive, not simply because of its royal connections, but because of the 10,000 or so fish which are taken out of its waters each year. Mind you, it takes deep pockets to fish a river like this, as a Dee rod can cost £200 a day. (It's all relative, I suppose. If you go to Norway, you could spend £2000 a day!)

But, seriously, don't be put off by sums like this. This is the real luxury end of the fly-fishing market and if you look round, you'll find there's much more affordable fishing about. For example, you could find yourself a small spate water which yields, say 30 fish a year. Now that may cost just a few pounds for a day's angling and, who knows, you could catch one of the 30!

Just as returns affect the price in fishing, so do names. Take the famous Junction Pool on the River Tweed at Kelso in the Borders. Anglers the length and breadth of Britain would give an arm, (though preferably not their casting one) and a leg for the chance to cast one solitary fly there, but fame doesn't come cheap, and here, you could pay thousands. That is if you ever got the opportunity, as rumour has it that it's fully booked for months, even years to come. At a place like this it might be a case of dead men's shoes if you're ever lucky enough to get on the waiting list.

Prices also vary according to the time of year. For example, there are some rivers that can be fished most of the year during the rod-season, but there are others that are really only worth bothering with at certain times. Some fish well in the spring, that is, they have a spring run of salmon, while others are better fished during the summer and autumn months. As a beginner, do make sure you find out if your chosen water has a 'better' time.

Most of us aren't in the position of waste money on hopeless fishing and you'll find that it pays to shop around to see what's available. Ask other anglers if they know of anything reasonable, or scan the adverts in a reputable fishing magazine. Bargains can be found. For example, one year we approached a local river owner and asked if we could take one rod for one day a week throughout the season. It cost

£100 for the year, which worked out at just a few pounds per day. On another occasion, up in Aberdeenshire, we made for the River Don, a highly respectable water, and paid £10 a head for several hours' joy. A fine spring salmon was landed; needless to say, it wasn't me that caught it!

Another good-value alternative can be to book an angling holiday, where fishing and hotel come as a package. It might mean sacrificing that trip to the sun, but if your chosen fishing place has a good atmosphere and you catch a salmon, you won't think twice about the delights of the Med. You'll fish to your heart's content, be well fed and watered and be safe in the knowledge that when you start your tale of woe about the one that got away, there will be no shortage of sympathetic ears! And when the holiday's over, you'll return, hopefully, not just with a bulging bag of fish, but a host of memories and a selection of new friends too.

Finally, before you get completely turned off by all this talk of renting and three-figure sums, I would suggest that one of the best ways a beginner can learn to fish for salmon is to join a local angling club. These associations own or rent some of the finest waters in Britain, though you generally have to live in the area to qualify for membership.

I remember I couldn't afford to splash out on fancy river fees when I first started fishing, so I joined an angling club in Carlisle and it turned out to be great value. For an annual fee of £40, I gained access to several miles of sound double-bank salmon fishing on the River Eden. It was particularly good for a beginner who didn't know many people and I was introduced to a whole team of other keen, helpful anglers who were more than happy to show me the ropes. I still can't afford to fish as much as I'd like on the bigger rivers and this year I hope to take an association ticket on the Border Esk. I'll have to buy it, though, having unfortunately failed to win the prize of a year's free fishing for the person who caught the first salmon on our local stretch of water! Mind you, there was a lot of competition since there are a great many good anglers in this neck of the woods.

Clubs are therefore great value for money and they're a wonderful way for a beginner to start to learn to fish. They do have their drawbacks, though. For instance, not everyone will be fly-fishing. Some will be spinning with wooden or metal lures, others use messier and smellier baits like worms and preserved pink and purple prawns. The purist won't approve of such methods being used anywhere near him. Frankly, as long as the beginner can cast his fly on his own little pool, who cares? Also, because they're such good value for money, clubs do tend to be popular and association banks can become quite crowded. However, looking on the bright side, if that does happen, at least the competition will spur you on and there will be lots of other like-minded folk around to lend whatever tackle you've forgotten or lost and to help you haul out that huge salmon if and when you catch him!

Assuming you do get your salmon, there will of course be much celebration, but try to keep it a dignified affair, (says she, who still whoops for joy on such occasions!) because, contrary to what people might think, an angler is not there solely to catch fish. Like the Renaissance man, the fisher embraces the completeness of the sport: nature, fresh air, the ripple of a stream and the peace of a mossy bank. Unlike someone we came across who was casting away in the middle of the river, while his partner sat quite happily on the gravel behind him, with Bruce Springsteen blaring out of a ghetto-blaster. I have nothing against Bruce Springsteen, in fact, he'd definitely be up there among the records I'd take to my desert island, but, there is a time and a place for everything, so I suggest that if you're the sort of person who hates silence, you should take up a different sport. Alternatively you could get yourself a Walkman and fish with headphones, or change your partner!

Above all, abide by the rules of the river. If it's a gentleman's agreement that a place is fly-only, as, for example, all the rivers in Sutherland are, then using a spinning bait or a prawn or any other means just isn't on, even if you own the whole shooting match. Be warned by the tale of the river owner who was prosecuted for poaching his own river. His wife had sent him out to catch a salmon for a lunch party he was having later that week and all day he'd fished a fly in vain so, in desperation as darkness fell, he carefully rowed himself out in a small boat, pushed a net over the side and cunningly scooped out a fish. Now you'd think that if you owned the water, you'd get away with one solitary salmon, but that's not what happened in this case. Against all the odds, he was seen and reported by a vigilant water watcher and instead of a fancy lunch, he found himself in a fine mess in court. Always stick to the rules — in the countryside, there's always someone who knows what's going on!

Although it's great to take home a salmon or two, I always tell myself that there's more to fishing than just catching fish. Take the story of the angler who died and found himself — well, it must been in heaven — for the day was mild, the wind was kind and a streamy river beckoned. Our fisher was even lucky enough to find a rather expensive fly-rod lying on the bank; so he waded in and got to work. First cast and the water boiled round the fly and there was a fish! He reeled in excitedly and the salmon came willingly, though almost too willingly, to the net. Next cast, a fish! He reeled in again and claimed his prize. And the next and the next! It seemed he just couldn't miss as each throw of the line produced a salmon. Half-an-hour later with 30 silvery offerings lying behind him on the bank, it suddenly dawned on him that he was bored. The challenge had gone, the excitement just wasn't there; in that moment, he realised to his horror that he wasn't in heaven. And if he wasn't in heaven, there was only one other place he could be!

The Salmon

The salmon is accounted the King of freshwater fish, and is ever bred in Rivers relating to the sea, yet so high or far from it as admits no tincture of salt or brackishness.

Isaak Walton, *The Compleat Angler*, 1653

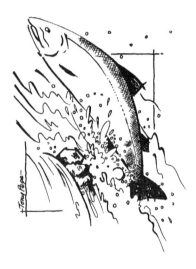

I remember the day clearly. It was fairly typical spring, Highland weather, slightly overcast and damp, with a hint of warmth promising better things to come. As always in Scotland, we'd breakfasted well and we arrived at the river, fuelled with the statutory porridge, kippers and oatcakes and fired with enthusiasm for the coming day. And what a day! First cast for my husband and bang! — there was a salmon on the end, a large, silvery, 15-pound beauty which tugged and strained at the end of his line. It danced angrily in and out of the water, making me fearful that this would be yet another one that got away. But despite the commotion, my husband, a fisher since the tender age of five, kept his nerve and eventually, after what seemed like a lifetime to me, but in

Two cracking salmon caught by Rod within five minutes at the Cassley Falls

reality was probably only 20 minutes or so, he called for the net and we landed it; our first fish of the year, lying sparkling in the grass.

It was caught on a two-inch Waddington, a large hairy fly, so I attached the same and climbed gingerly down the bank. Two minutes later and my line tightened as a huge spring fish came leaping out of the pool. More out of the water than in, it careered up and down and all I could hear was the splashing of the water and my husband beside me, muttering darkly, 'I don't like it, I don't like it!' I didn't like it either — the line suddenly slackened and it had gone! What looked like a 17-pound fish, the biggest I would have ever have caught was not to be mine.

'What did I do wrong?!', I asked in anguish.

'Nothing, really,' he replied, 'but you should have dropped your rod-tip when he leapt out of the water. It wouldn't have caused such a strain on the line.'

Now he tells me, I thought, rather unkindly. However, forewarned is forearmed and the next salmon was a certainty, an 11-pounder that I placed proudly on the bank behind us. That morning we caught five of these royal fish; four for him and one for me, with three more hooked but lost. A morning to remember for a fly-fisher, as such times are rare and all the more magical for being so.

Yes, there's no getting away from it; to catch a salmon is something special since there's something about this fish that sets it apart from other, lesser ones. Maybe it's the look; the rose-pink flesh clothed in silver that seems so inviting on a plate. Or perhaps it's the fact that salmon smacks of special occasion. Wherever it's served, be it at weddings or wakes, races or regattas, and however it comes, dressed in aspic, smoked, or even straight from the tin, there's always a hint of luxury. Oh, there's no doubt that the salmon has star-quality and that's despite the fact that these days it's readily obtainable, with numerous salmon farms providing a constant supply for the fishmonger. More than that, the unthinkable has now happened and a pound of farmed salmon can often cost less than its poor relation, the cod. We're not quite at the days of salmon and chips, but almost!

Hundreds of years ago it was cheap and plentiful too. Then, like the oyster, the salmon was an everyday food, so common that many estate workers would have it written into their terms of employment that they wouldn't get it to eat more than twice a week, 'Thou shalt not catch salmon more than twice a week'! If only today's fey fisher could have something similar written into his contract! For the sad fact is, fellow beginners, that although there may be plenty of farmed salmon about, the fish that you and I are after, the river or wild salmon, seems now to be increasingly elusive.

It's definitely a case of the good old days and it seems to me that wherever I go, there are fed-up fishers bemoaning their luck and talking wistfully of the past. Talk to any seasoned angler and he'll recall times when catches were plentiful, when all it took was a few, fruitful hours by the river and every member of the family, Aunt Peggy and Uncle Tom included, would return home with a couple of salmon each. These days, I have to confess that a couple a year would be a wonderful thing! And the further you go back, the better it appeared to be. For example, take this report from The Field magazine a century ago, which refers to one week's fishing on the River Eden in Cumbria. This was one stretch of water that obviously escaped the onslaught of the industrial revolution!

A salmon of 56lb was killed here last Friday. On Wednesday, Mr E.L.Hough, solicitor, killed in the Crosby water nine fish, (weighing over 200lb), and on Friday eight more. A number of fish were landed in the Linstock water. Mr H Ford Barclay of Monkhams Essex caught eight, the heaviest a very fine fresh-run fish of 41lb, Mr Bland, eleven, six of which were over 20lb. In the lower portion of Rickerby water, Mr MacInnes, MP, the proprietor, killed six fish last week, the heaviest 29lb, Mr J. MacInnes landed five. At Eden Banks, Mr R.F. Hall of Liverpool has killed fifteen salmon in six days...and so on and so on!

A hundred years later and how times have changed. Two years

ago, I fished the selfsame river every week from February right through to October, and caught one solitary salmon there. I was lucky though, as some people caught nothing at all. It was a depressingly blank year and it could be that 20th century fishers are less proficient than their Victorian counterparts, but I somehow doubt it.

So what is happening? Why are river catches so erratic these days and why, indeed, has the combined world catch of salmon declined by more than 50% over the last 20 years? Returns have been halved on many rivers and the cry among today's anglers is, 'Where are the fish?'

Where are they indeed? It would be easy simply to blame pollution for killing or driving stocks away, for our rivers haven't been especially well treated by modern man. But, there again, as people become more environmentally aware, it's a fact that many waters are cleaner than they've ever been. Rivers like the Thames and the Tyne, which were formerly too full of chemicals and sewage for the salmon's liking, have once again become habitable. Pollution is certainly one cause for the apparent decline in numbers of wild salmon, but there are other reasons too. For example, large-scale fishing at Atlantic feeding grounds or over-enthusiastic commercial netting at river mouths. All of these have contributed to the depletion of numbers coming up rivers. Even the innocent-looking grey seal, which has increased in frightening numbers around our coastline, stands accused of greedily working his way through precious fish stocks.

On the other hand, there are those fishers who'll tell you that the salmon are still there in reasonable numbers, but the reason that they're not appearing on the list of fish returns is that they're simply not being caught, and they're simply not being caught because they're changing their pattern of behaviour. In other words, the theory is that wild salmon are still returning to British rivers in fairly large numbers, but these days they're coming when they're least expected, that is, in the close season, in the winter months, when rod-fishing isn't allowed. Has this formidable fish found the ultimate way to outwit the poor old angler? Cunning and unpredictable, I've been reading up on this King of the river.

A salmon, the experts tell me, comes into the world as a tiny egg laid deep down in the gravel of a stream or river. The egg can take many weeks to hatch, but when it does, it becomes an elvin, which is a tiny fish with a yolksac to provide nourishment. When the yolksac is absorbed it becomes a fry. At the end of a year, this fry has become what's known as a parr, which is a little fish of between three and five inches which feeds on aquatic life such as insects and worms, surviving by avoiding other predators like birds and bigger fish. It eventually takes on a silver colour and now it's known as a smolt, ready to leave its birthplace and migrate to the sea. If it stayed, it wouldn't survive. If you think of it, few rivers could provide enough food for thousands of full-grown salmon, so the smolt head for the saltwater and the rich feeding grounds in the ocean.

There, in this new kingdom, the salmon eats voraciously, using sharp teeth to feed on smaller fish and plankton, so that by the end of the first year the small fish that left the British shore can be 20 times or more its original size. But although a salmon will mature in the sea, it cannot spawn there. Reproduction can only be done in fresh water, so at some stage it must return home. Not just to any old home however, for a salmon will head for the self-same river in which it it was spawned, and to almost the same spot. This returning to spawn is called a run and some rivers have a spring run and others an autumn one. Indeed, some have a run all year round, but whenever the fish comes back, it'll have to wait for late autumn or winter before it's are ready to lay its eggs.

So they return. And swimming with great determination through the sea at great speeds, they have one sole purpose, to find their native water. How they manage to work their way across seas and rivers remains one of nature's great mysteries, but some scientists think that their sense of direction is connected to magnetic centres in their brain. Another theory is that salmon have a good sense of smell and that each river estuary may have its own distinctive scent, which guides the fish in. Whatever it is, following these finely-tuned instincts and surviving ocean hazards like the seal and the fisherman's net, the salmon reach the mouth of their home river and here the last stretch begins.

Upstream they go, racing along, for these fish have amazing stamina. Their great tails and fins have been developed by strenuous exercise at sea, and it's this strength which allows them to tackle the most daunting river obstacle. They swim with great determination against the current, carefully avoiding lurking nets, resisting lures and painstakingly negotiating rocky pools and waterfalls. Salmon are incredible jumpers and experts have pointed out that their Latin name suits them well. Salmo Salar. Salar means the leaper.

Nowhere have I seen this more clearly demonstrated than on the falls of the Rivers Cassley and Shin in Sutherland, which stretch up in stages 50 feet and more. Out of the still water, the fish enter the roaring foam and then hurl themselves towards a platform several feet higher, before being washed back into the pool. Nothing daunted, they valiantly regroup, some trying for days, even weeks in their quest to reach the spawning grounds several miles up the glen. Here, jumps of six or seven feet are quite common, but the highest leap for a salmon, recorded in Scotland, is some 12 feet. How they manage to project themselves upwards with such amazing force is a mystery to most of us, but Isaak Walton maintained in 1653 that they did so by putting their tails in their mouths and catapulting themselves up!

The lucky ones eventually reach their destination and it is here, in the gravelly spawning grounds, that the hard work pays off. During their life at sea, salmon tend to swim in shoals, but on entering the freshwater, they will generally have paired up, the males known as cocks, the females hens. In the shallow water, the hen digs a hole in the river bed and deposits her eggs and these are then fertilised by the cock. And that, I'm afraid, is sadly the end for most of them; after spawning, around three-quarters of all salmon will die. Only a handful remain to return to the sea and, exhausted, these hardy survivors make downstream and the cycle starts again.

Those which do survive are known as kelts and if you catch one, which is quite easily done as they come downriver in early spring, the law and fishing etiquette, insist it must be returned to the water at once. You can't eat it, so you may as well be magnanimous. Putting a kelt back is one thing; recognising one is often not quite so easy. The textbook definition is a thin, blackened, often diseased fish, but a kelt can be well mended. That is, by the time you catch it, it may be halfway back down the river again and have regained some of its original silver colour and weight. In short, it can be difficult to distinguish from a fresh salmon, especially for the inexperienced.

I've caught a couple of kelts in the few years that I've been fishing and can testify that it's not easy to work out if they're to be kept or put back. I remember being rather suspicious one day when a fish rather half-heartedly took my fly and then proceeded to flop about in the water. It was springtime and, had it been a fresh-run salmon it should by rights have been straining at the leash. I brought it to the bank, but by this stage, my husband was also looking dubious. It was my first fish of the year and I was all for keeping it of course, so I was trying to convince myself, and Rod, that it wasn't what we thought it was! It wasn't blackened, in fact it was quite silvery. True, it was a little thin, but that's not a crime is it? Its fate, and mine, were finally decided when we pulled back the gills and found a host of maggots nestling there. A sure sign of a kelt. Back it went, to live another day and, I hope, another season.

It's certainly a difficult area, for the question of a kelt can be an emotive issue. Is it, or is it not? And how unfair on the fish, if the only way to find out is when the angler cuts it open on the kitchen table and sees the flesh, pale, dry and unappetising. I've tasted a kelt and pretty disgusting it was too. It was billed as freshly-grilled salmon steak with parsley butter, but when it came it was almost grey in colour. I complained of the cardboard taste and the waiter got quite indignant. 'We've just bought this fresh from a local fisher', he said. Obviously, someone had pulled a fast one. So the advice is, if you're uncertain, then put it back. Because, one thing's for sure, if you doubt your own fish, everyone else will too! It's a heartbreaking decision, I know, especially if you're a beginner and this is your first salmon, but, believe me, you'll feel infinitely worse if you kill it, only to find that it's inedible. Meanwhile, if you really want to avoid having to make that vital judgement, confine your fishing to the summer and autumn months; expert opinion has is that by the beginning of May, most kelts will have descended the river and reached the sea and sensibly be well out of the enthusiastic angler's way.

Another term you will come across in salmon fishing is a grilse, and this is certainly edible. A grilse is a young salmon which has returned to spawn after just one sea winter. Now it may weight just a few pounds, but if you're lucky enough to catch one covered in sea-lice, it'll mean it's just come into the fresh water from the sea and you'll be guaranteed one of the tastiest meals in the world!

That, briefly, is the salmon, a fish that's been studied by naturalists and anglers for centuries and still remains a source of mystery. The one really fascinating fact I picked up in all my research is that a when a grown salmon comes back to the river to spawn, it doesn't actually feed there. So how on earth does it survive? Well, it appears that what it does is to stock up whilst at sea, taking on board enough food to last it the many months it will need to work its way up river. It's an amazing thought really, if you imagine the distance a salmon may have to travel, in some cases, thousands of miles, and the amount of energy it must use in battling its way upstream. And all that without eating after its return to the river. It just shows what determined and remarkable fish they are.

There must be a reason for their abstinence in the river and one theory is that it's nature's way of protecting the species. Just imagine if a 20-pound salmon were allowed to feed as voraciously on its return to its native freshwater as it did in the ocean. Because of the sheer size and numbers involved, it would soon clean out the pools and thus jeopardise the survival of its own species.

'But', you're probably asking, as I did when I first had this explained to me, 'if a salmon doesn't look for food in the river, then why does it go for the fisherman's fly?' There are various explanations, some more romantic than others. The salmon, they say, is a bad-tempered creature who snaps irritably and aggressively at anything dangled before him. Another, rather more scientific reason offered is that the salmon takes the lure out of habit, the feathered freshwater morsel stirring a faint feeding memory of some tasty titbit from the sea. To my beginner's mind this sounds like a plausible and more inviting explanation.

Whichever reason you favour though, what is generally acknowledged is that water temperature has a great influence on whether or not a salmon takes. Now, on this matter, there have been great theses written by learned men, so I won't attempt to comment further. Suffice to say that we beginners should know that we're more likely to catch a fish when the air is warmer than the water.

Indeed, you'll find that there are all sorts of theories in salmon fishing and some are nicely straightforward. But it's always the same; you make certain statements about this very worthy adversary and, damn it, he does something completely different! In fact, it's an unpredictable sport all round and you'll find that there's really never a right way or a definite reason for anything, and just when you think you've found one, something happens to confound it all. I'm afraid that when it comes to catching a salmon on the fly, it's all a case of, 'you should have been here yesterday... last week... even tomorrow!' Alas, never today! As in the Fisher's Lament, a ditty found written in books and pinned up in fishing huts. It's a rhyme that you will soon identify with.

Sometimes ower* early,	*over*
Sometimes ower late,	
Sometimes nae water,	
Sometimes a spate.	
Sometimes ower calm	
Sometimes ower clear.	
There's aye* something wrang*,	*always, wrong*
When I'm fishing here!	

Tackle

A stick and a string with a fly at one end and a fool at the other.

With apologies to George Bernard Shaw

So you still want to take up fly-fishing? Well, first of all, don't rush out and buy all the gear. Fishing tackle as it's called, isn't cheap, and let's face it, until you've tried the sport, you don't know whether you'll like it. Besides which, there are hundreds of weird and wonderful angling terms and unless the beginner knows his sinker from his floater or his Garry Dog from his Stoat's Tail, sorting out what's important and what isn't can be a minefield.

If you've booked yourself into a reputable fishing school, they'll almost certainly provide the basic equipment on which to practice. If, however, you're being taught by friends, then do try to borrow whatever's required for the first few trips to the river. It shouldn't be an impossible request. Fishers are great hoarders and I've yet to meet one who didn't have at least twice as much tackle as required! A few lessons later, when you've decided that you too are hooked, that's the time to take yourself along to the sporting or tackle shop and start buying.

I have to warn you here, that for a beginner, even for a much practised shopper like I am, this can be a daunting experience and in my pre-marriage days, I recall passing this dusty-fronted shop, its window draped variously with nets and green rubber; its counter covered in gaudy, mean-looking hooks, its shelves stacked with what looked suspiciously like bales of washing line. What was it all for, and who would need it? Vets? Scientists?

It was only when I was introduced to fishing that I discovered what went on behind those mysterious doors. Gradually, it became quite clear. From the smartest London tackle shop, with the latest, lightest, foolproof net, to the smallest Highland hut where a ghillie's wife ran up home-made flies at 50p a time, a fascinating world of rods, reels, wellies and waders had opened up. To be honest, the only thing I still find a little hard to come to terms with is all the hardware! Fishing tackle is more often than not sold alongside hunting and shooting stuff, and I still find the rifles and shotguns a bit intimidating. I know that country folk are supposed to be well used to that sort of thing, but I grew up believing that the only place for a gun was in a Western.

However, hardware aside, there's no doubt that browsing in a tackle shop is a delightful pastime. The only drawback is that, once inside, there's a great temptation to spend, spend, spend. But, just as clothes don't make a fisher, neither does the tackle! So take your time and don't rush into anything. Better still, take along an angling friend to help you decide. And before getting carried away, don't forget that it's fly-fishing stuff that you're after. Tackle for any other sort of angling is quite unsuitable, so if in doubt, ask the assistant, for there should be no shortage of help in a good tackle shop. Most of it is well meaning, as the folk behind the counter are often great fishers themselves and can become great friends, delighted to advise on the type of equipment, as well as giving all the local gossip like the height of nearby rivers and the number of salmon being caught. Just beware of the odd unscrupulous salesman, (though I've yet to meet one) who can and will dump on the novice the stock he's not been able to shift to those who know better.

So, first get your rod, and again, do make sure it's the right one. A rod for sea-fishing or for spinning is no good to someone who wants to catch a salmon on the fly. As a beginner, you'll be relieved to know that one rod will do, although as you improve, you may find yourself buying another, perhaps something heavier for winter or early spring, or a lighter one for the summer.

If you can afford it, that is, because unfortunately rods aren't cheap! True, you might get a non-name for £50 or £60, but on the other hand people have been known to pay £500 or more for something really fancy. Now I have neither the budget nor the inclination to pay such a sum for a rod and as a beginner, neither should you. Just buy the best you can afford, because it's probably a false economy to do otherwise. After all, who wants something that's going to snap in two the first time it's used? If it's any guide, my first fly-rod cost £100, which six years ago seemed more than enough to pay. One final thought on price, if you're really hard-up and in need of a bargain, then ask the shop if they sell second-hand equipment. My husband bought a used rod ten years ago and it's still going strong. But do be cautious on that one — as they say, buyer beware!

So let me tell you something about your rod. Basically, most salmon fly-rods are double-handed, which means you use both hands when you fish with them. British salmon fly-rods vary in length and can be anything from 11ft 6inches upwards, though the average size seems to be around 15 feet. Incidentally, rods are known in the trade as 'footers', so a 15-foot rod is simply referred to as a '15 footer'.

Your fly-rod comes in several parts so that it can be easily carried and stored. There are generally three parts which slot together. To protect them, these parts are kept in a covering called a sleeve. Some sleeves are made of canvas, others are of plastic, leather, or even metal — but obviously, the more rigid the sleeve, the more protection there is for the rod.

Yes, today's fly-fisher has a relatively easy life when it comes to the tackle used to catch salmon for in times past, a day by the river would really sort out the men from the boys. Stiff, heavy rods made of split-cane sounded like real back-breakers, veritable instruments of torture, which according to folklore needed a man and a boy to carry them to the water, and an even sturdier soul to fish with them. One such is our friend Joe, who's a bit of a traditionalist and uses an enormous greenheart rod with a piece of steel down the middle, which belonged to his grandfather and which he inherited along with a collection of beautifully-tied, classic flies. Joe will flog away with this thing all day and by dusk, he'll be aching like mad. However, he maintains it's the proper way to fish!

It may be that he's right and I'm all for tradition, but I've tried one of these antiques and lasted all of ten minutes before retiring defeated to the bank. They're certainly beautiful to look at, and I would love to have one hanging on my wall at home, but I wouldn't recommend a beginner to learn to fish with anything remotely resembling one of these since it will put you off for life!

What a novice needs is something lightweight, flexible and strong and these days there's certainly no shortage of choice on the market. Fashioned from carbon-fibre and fibreglass, there are dozens of makes and styles available and the beauty is that they're easy to handle whilst being tough enough to take the strain of an energetic salmon. Be careful with the really light ones though — I'll go into this later in the book; suffice to say that a drop from a height, or a knock against something hard can easily shatter a carbon-fibre rod and that makes for an expensive day's fishing!

So, what size of rod should the beginner go for? As I mentioned earlier, salmon fly-rods come in all sorts of lengths, the theory being, I suppose, that the longer the rod is, the greater the distance you can throw the line. I've seen 20 foot rods in use, but as a novice, you'll definitely want something more modest. Several professionals I've talked to say they would always start a beginner on a 15 footer, but when I was learning to fish I started on a 12½ footer and after a few months prac-

*My own rod in its cloth sleeve
Below: Reel with line and the
handy protective case*

tice, I moved to a 14 footer, which I've since stayed with and which seems to be a good length for someone my height, (five-foot-four and a half inches). In comparison, my sister-in-law Lesley, who's a few inches taller, uses a 15 footer, as does my husband, who's six-foot-two.

As for the make, there are dozens on the market, and you'll probably end up getting quite confused. But if you really can't decide what to buy, it may be that a good tackle shop will let you try one out at the river, supervised of course since you wouldn't test drive a car if you didn't know how to drive!

I used borrowed rods for about six months before finally deciding to buy my own and I can recommend this as a cheap and cheerful way of doing things since it gave me a chance to see what I liked and what I didn't. When I eventually felt that family and friends had had enough of my scrounging, I decided it was time to splash out. So, I did the tour of all the local tackle shops, cautiously handled dozens of makes and still couldn't decide, but then I came across a Japanese make, not an expensive one and certainly not a great classic, but it's flexible, which I like, and it casts a good line. The only thing that seems to offend the more traditional fishers is that it's got the logo 'Fish X-Citer' written all over the side, which is a bit over the top when you're spending a leisurely day by the river, but it suits me and it did manage to hook a salmon on its very first outing. So who cares!

So you've chosen your rod and now you'll need a reel to hold your line; the right sort, of course. Remember you want a fly-reel, not a spinning-reel or any other type. And again, go for the best you can afford, as a good one could last years, if not a lifetime. I've noticed some of the more senior fishers using heavy, cranky old things which look almost prehistoric, but they seem to catch salmon alright.

Now, any fisher will tell you that a good reel isn't cheap and can cost anything from £40 upwards. Most fly-fishers I know have two or three to hold different types of line and also have a 'spare' handy, but a cheaper way of doing it is to buy one reel and several spools, which is the bit in the middle of the reel that holds the line and backing.

However many spools or reels are bought, the advice from the experts is that the reel must always be in balance with the rod. As a beginner, I was told time and time again that balance is half the battle in good casting and really, it does makes sense. Using a small, modern reel on an old-fashioned, heavy rod, would be daft. Likewise, a small, lightweight carbon-fibre rod would be next to useless weighed down by a large, metal reel. So make sure it's the right one for the rod, and that it also fits the reel-seat. Your tackle shop assistant should keep you right on this.

You've now got the rod and the reel and next you need some line which is is basically a long length of plastic-coated thread. It's expensive, at £25 or more for a length but, treated with care, it should last for several years. And again, when buying line, think of balance, since line comes in different weights and it's important to get the right one. If you look just above the butt of the rod, you'll see a number which refers to the recommended weight of line, but if you're still in doubt, ask the tackle shop assistant.

Line also comes in different types, and here you must decide what sort of fishing you plan to do. Anglers out in early spring when rivers are high and cold often use what's called a sinking line, and this is line which does just that; it sinks down into the water to take the fly to the fish. But if it's late spring or summer, when temperatures are rising and water levels are lower, fishers will usually put on a floating line, which floats on the surface of the water. Then there are other sorts of line, such as the intermediate or the sink-tip variety and it's often difficult and confusing to know which to use. So let's make it simple and say that a beginner will generally and hopefully learn to fish with a floating line. It's so much easier to pull 25 metres of wet plastic off the surface of a pool than it is off the bottom! Incidentally, I would advise that a novice should start with a double-taper line — just ask the assistant again!

So, you now have your line and when I first ventured out into the water, 25 metres seemed more than long enough to deal with a fish of any size. However, imagine what happens when a 20-pound salmon snatches the fly and goes angrily tearing down river at a rate of knots, that is, it decides to run. If that occurs, the line will rapidly spool off the reel and will almost certainly prove too short. So to give you that extra length, what you now need is some backing and this is thin, plaited nylon, which goes onto the reel before the line to provide an extra 50 to 100 metres, should the fish so wish to take it. Since a spool of backing costs just a few pounds, it is, in effect, a cheap means of lengthening the line.

The next piece of casting equipment is nylon; the link between line and fly which is often referred to as a cast or leader. Nylon is needed to carry the fly out into the water. It's supposed to be almost invisible, though whether the salmon is that easily duped, I'm not so sure!

There are different makes and breaking strains of nylon, and here again, you must get the right weight. If it's too light, it won't take the fly out properly or, worse still, it'll snap under the strain of a big fish. Likewise, if it's too heavy, it may not allow the fly to swim properly in the water. So how does a fisher know what weight to use? Well, very simply, he should gauge the strength of nylon by the river conditions and by the size of fish he hopes to catch. If it's any help, I've been told it's always better to overestimate rather than underestimate. However, here's a general guide of what I was advised to use when fishing for salmon.

If it's early spring and I'm using large flies in deep water, a stiff, strong nylon is the order of the day to carry the heavy fly through the wind; so a breaking strain of 20 pounds may be used. Then, as the year goes on, it's possible to come down in size and in late summer, when fishing low water with tiny flies, I sometimes go as light as eight pounds, but don't forget that on days like this, the angler always runs the risk of the nylon being broken, either by a heavy fish, or a jagged rock.

Nylon comes on a spool and costs just a few pounds and unless you're particularly heavy-handed, a spool should last all season. The alternative for those lazy or wealthy fishers is to buy a ready-made nylon cast, but these are pricey, so be warned! A note here: these casts sometimes have what's known as a dropper hanging from them and this is simply another piece of nylon attached to the main leader which allows you to fish two flies in one pool. A lot of fun and sometimes a lot of fish can be had with a dropper, but they're certainly not to be recommended for beginners because they tend to wind themselves round the rod and bring all sorts of trouble. I can assure you that as a novice, you'll have enough problems dealing with one fly flapping about, let alone two! Believe me, even the experienced can find it a nightmare.

My father-in-law told me how he was once using two flies in high summer when a salmon took the tail-fly, and seconds later, another grabbed the dropper-fly. Well, both fish started to pull the line in different directions and he couldn't make head nor tail of it. Suffice to say, he nearly broke the rod and he lost both fish. And Tommy's a man with 50 year's experience!

And so to the fly itself and, as we know by now, the game fisher does not have to go round in search of juicy bluebottles to attach to the end of his line. Basically, salmon flies are artificial lures, hairy hooks — often brightly coloured — which float on or merge with the water to attract the fish and, for me, this is one of the best bits of all; studying the hundreds of shapes, sizes and colours and choosing from delightful names like the Hairy Mary, the Willie Gunn, the Collie Dog and the Tadpole. Or the more graphic labels like the Munro Killer, the General Practitioner and the Muddler. They are fashioned out of feather, silk and hair, which is tied carefully to barbed hooks, and they come in shades of red, yellow, blue, green and black with hints of silver tinsel across the body. Some are up to two inches long and brass-weighted, others are a quarter that size and as light as a real fly. There are boxes and boxes of different patterns to get lost in, so how do you know which one to use?

Very simply, the size of the fly depends on the temperature of the water. So, when it's really cold, big flies of two inches and more will be needed. Then when summer comes, you can go down to lightweight flies of half-an-inch or less. And there are different types of fly. For example, the single-hooked ordinary fly has obviously one hook, the double has two and the treble has three, and so on. Then there's what's known as the tube fly; this is where the body of the fly can be separated from the hook. All of these are used in salmon fishing, and you'll need to take advice as to which size and which hook is best for the water and the weather.

As far as colour or pattern is concerned, I shall be highly controversial here and suggest that for a beginner, it doesn't really matter that much. Frankly, there are so many types around that until you know the ropes, you may as well just choose a colour you like the look of. As long as the size is right, there's probably as good a chance as any of catching a fish on a yellow and silver as there is on a blue and black. The well known fisher and writer Dr Malcolm Greenhalgh, whose brain I picked whilst writing this book, tells me that everyone should have a 'What is it?' fly in their collection. You needn't necessarily know the name, but as long as it's the correct size, it may hook a fish and he should know because he's caught a fair few in his time. Finally there's always the old adage: 'A bright fly for a bright day, a dull fly for a dull day'. That's certainly worked a couple of times for me, so I suppose it's as good a gauge as any.

Moving onto other accessories, flies will need something to be kept in; left loose in the bottom of a tackle bag, they'll get tangled up with all the other stuff and you'll run the risk of pricking yourself when you delve deep inside. So a plastic or metal fly-box will do fine for this purpose, preferably one lined with foam, so the hooks don't move and become entangled. You'll probably find you end up with several boxes before too long but so far as the salmon fisher is concerned, there can never be too many. It's also wise to keep the cold-weather flies apart from the summer flies; the tubes from the trebles and so on. I warn you though, once you start collecting flies, there's no way back. I'm just a newcomer, with maybe 30 or 40, but a friend of ours has literally hundreds, which he keeps in drawers and mounted in display cases on walls. He brings out a few at a time and lovingly takes them down to the river for their annual wetting.

To carry fly-box, reel and line, you'll need a tackle-bag and this can be made of anything sturdy that doesn't particularly mind having the odd run-in with water. I've a wicker fishing basket which hangs over my shoulder, and my husband uses a large, canvas hold-all, but really, it's whatever makes you happy and whatever you can afford. It could be as little as £10, on the other hand, you could pay £100 for a fancy, leather job. Whatever it is though, make sure it's fairly plain as you don't want to spend precious fishing time disentangling line from the numerous hooks and straps on your bag!

Then, when you catch that fish, you'll need a salmon net and again, go for a good one. Nets take a lot of punishment when caught on bushes or sharp rocks and you want something that's going to stand the test of time. I've had my net for several years now and it's still going strong. I know it really doesn't see that much action, but it's been bashed about on numerous fishing trips, used as an impromptu wading staff and to carry anything but fish, so it's really not doing too badly!

Rod's tackle bag above my own definition of the same!
Below: Salmon net. Note the stone to steady it in the water.

Remember also that salmon nets tend to be pretty large and unwieldy, so if space is at a premium at home, you may like to consider a collapsible one, but one which doesn't decide to give way at the wrong moment! If you're forgetful, like I am, you may like to consider a Gye net with a sling, which means you won't be separated from your net at a critical time.

One further point here, you'll sometimes hear ghillies or older fishers talk of a gaff; this is a contraption used to hook the fish and pull it out of the water. I understand it's an old-fashioned method, once very popular with anglers, but it's not one that I would want to use, as it seems rather crude. Hugh Falkus says in his book on salmon fishing, 'Why violate a creature as beautiful as an Atlantic salmon by sticking a meat hook into him?'

You may also hear talk of a tailer; this is a loop of wire that tightens round the fish's tail and lifts it out of the water. It's good to know what these things are, but as a beginner, I should avoid both the above and stick to the net.

And so to the smaller, but often vital, bits of tackle. Included in your kit should be a small pair of scissors to cut line and nylon, but make sure that they've got a rounded, safety edge.

I also carry a box of matches, partly because I live in hope of being able to light a fire to barbecue freshly-caught fish, but more importantly, the emery on the side on a matchbox is good for keeping hook-points nice and sharp. I also carry a safety-pin which is great for unpicking wind knots, (more on that later, too) and a torch because it's very easy to get carried away by the river and forget about time. I also carry some insect-repellent to keep the midges at bay, if such a thing be possible! A small flask of something suitably warming is always useful for bribing bored partners or other fishers. Of course, if it is for you, then look on it as being purely medicinal. It's good to have in reserve and, who knows, it may be the perfect thing to toast the fish with at the end of the day.

Finally, you'll need something to carry that fish home in, won't you? Now the proper name for this piece of equipment is not a bag, but a bass, which is a salmon-shaped bag, usually made of straw, or hessian. Note here, if you're really stuck, it's possible to improvise with a plastic bag or, if it's really a whopper, a black bin-liner, but whatever's used, it makes sense to cover the fish at once, to protect it from sun and insects and other greedy souls.

A friend recalls how he was fishing the Dee one spring night when he landed a lovely, silvery, ten pound salmon. While admiring his catch, he heard a splash and was assured by the ghillie that the fish were most certainly on the take and that he should get back to the water and carry on the good work. So, gently laying his prize on the bank, he returned to the river, brimming with confidence to try to repeat his success. Well, he was halfway across the river and just getting into his stride, when there was a snuffle and a scuffle and our friend turned round to see a wild-eyed otter dragging his salmon up the bank into some neighbouring woods. The commotion and the panic as fisher and ghillie stumbled noisily out of the river and chased salmon and otter up the bank had to be seen and heard to be believed! You'll be relieved to hear he did get his fish back, but not quite in pristine condition.

So, watch your fish and watch your tackle, because in fishing just as in television, you never quite know who's watching you!

Clothing

Fishing is a delusion entirely surrounded by liars in old clothes.

Don Marquis

Clothes don't make a fisher

I'd love to say that clothes don't really matter to me, but of course they do, especially in my job. From time to time, after what I'd reckoned was a fairly serious programme, I'd force myself to look at the duty log to see what phone calls the broadcast had evoked. Were they complaining about bias on a serious, political issue; about accuracy on a certain set of figures, or the weight of a lead story? More often than not, many of the calls would be about delivery and appearance. 'Didn't like her yellow blouse, not her colour!' (Mr Smith, Woking) 'Enjoyed the report on the whales and, by the way, can you tell me where she buys her earrings?' (Mrs Brown, Kilsyth) Complete strangers still stop me in the street and tell me which outfits suit and which don't. I suppose I should be grateful that they stillbother to notice! Then there followed the dreaded 'F' factor and the whole debate about short skirts and legs. 'She's got astronauts legs, hockey-player's legs, she should cover them up in thick black tights', suggested some kindly members of the press. Probably right too, although I'd never really thought about it until then.

Well, I'm relieved to tell you that while clothes may help to make a presenter, they don't make a man and they certainly don't make an angler. So if you have this idea of the archetypal game-fisher in his statutory plus-twos and tweed cap, then think again. Oh yes, I do know folk who make sure they dress for the part and buy the right makes and styles but when you start to look around, they're not necessarily the most successful fishers.

A fellow newscaster tells me how, many moons ago, he decided to take up the sport as an antidote to the stresses and strains of television life. For two years, he threw himself wholeheartedly into the affair, buying all the right country clothes, all the proper tackle and dutifully went fishing, fishing, fishing for months on end. The fact that for two years he caught nothing, nay, didn't even have a single, solitary bite, didn't seem to deter him until one day when he was out with his family on a small river in the West Country.

Impromptu fishing on the Cassley. Ignore the attire!

'It's not fair. You can see the fish lying at the other side of the river,' he grumbled, 'and that's where I need to cast my line, but I can't get across there in these waders and this jacket's all wrong for the job. In fact I simply don't have the right clothes to fish in and that's why I never catch anything!' As he spoke, there was a loud whistle and a young man sauntered along the bank, casually dressed in a pair of cut-off jeans, a woolly jumper full of holes and a pair of battered wellies. Over his shoulder was an antiquated-looking rod, and he was carrying three large salmon. I'm afraid my colleague was so demoralised that he sold his fishing clothes and tackle and never fished again!

I've seen similar incidents with groups of us all flogging away on a fancy river in our regulation jackets and waders and catching absolutely nothing; then along comes a local, dressed as if he's out for an afternoon stroll, and proceeds on the first cast to hook a whopping great fish! It just goes to show that as far as looks go, it doesn't matter what you wear. Comfort is another thing and we'll go into that later, but as a beginner, you don't want to spend money on anything until you are convinced that you like the sport. So, if this is your first time by the river, look in the wardrobe and see if you can simply cobble something together. If it's chilly, a couple of warm tee-shirts, a pair of corduroy trousers, a thick woolly jumper and some warm socks will do fine. Beg, borrow or steal a waterproof jacket and hat if you don't have any, add some wellies and you're ready to go.

If the interest grows, then is the time to invest in some decent fishing clothes, and by decent, I mean warm and protective. True, there are glorious, dry summer days to be had by the river, but I have to be honest, in my experience when fishing for salmon, they're few and far between, so my advice is to prepare to take on the elements and plan for wind, rain and snow. I like this piece of Victorian advice, which I spotted in *Salmon, Trout and Sea-Trout* magazine.

When fishing in extreme conditions, leave the river every half hour and check your lower limbs. If they are scarlet, it is safe to re-enter the river; if blue, it is deemed unwise to continue, for to do so would result in loss of one, if not both, legs and it is wise to wait until circulation has returned.

So where to start to avoid such a catastrophe? Well, a beginner should buy clothing that's practical, comfortable and recommended. Take advice from other fishers and find out what sort of kit they suggest. The chances are, they'll probably start with a jacket A decent jacket can last for years and judging by some of the worn, torn specimens paraded on river banks, many obviously do! People get very attached to their old coats and I suppose there's a certain inverted country snobbery about not wearing something that's obviously brand spanking new. Rather like blue jeans, which get better and better the more faded and torn they become, a fishing jacket looks all the more desirable for its watery battle scars.

As for the style, that's very much a personal thing, but when you start looking round, you'll find that outdoor jackets are all much of a muchness, though the most popular ones do seem to be the green, waxed types. They vary in price and a well-known brand name could be £60 to £100 or more, but there are some good, cheaper, 'non-names' on the market for half the cost, so do look around. Somehow, I've ended up

Bad weather fishing on the Cassley — at least my head is warm

with two. One from a tackle shop, the other from a game fair, but I've seen quite a few bargains in chain stores and in Sunday magazines, so it's worth keeping an eye open.

Jackets come in all sorts of sizes and lengths and the choice depends on what sort of fishing you plan to do. For example, long jackets protect legs from rain and wind, and they're fine for winter or for fishing from the bank or in shallow water, but obviously they're not so good for wading in deep water. Shorter jackets are great in the summer as they're cool and airy, but, on the other hand, they don't give much protection in the winter. So, which one do you go for? Well, if I were choosing now, with all of my six year's experience behind me, I'd opt for something in-between, a middle length which sheds water onto the waders and not above them. I'd also choose something light. The fisher buying in the depths of winter might be tempted to go for the heaviest, warmest garment he can find, but that isn't going to be much use if the weather improves and the work heats up. Don't forget, you can always put on extra layers underneath. A fleecy detachable lining, a padded body-warmer, or even an extra jumper will do fine, but it's not so easy to make a heavy jacket lighter. One last thought when choosing: do make sure your jacket's got plenty of pockets, the more the merrier for a fisher, because we all need somewhere to put our fly-boxes, sweets, tissues, flask etc.

The next thing is a hood or a hat and this is vital as far as I'm concerned. Vital, not only for warmth in winter, but also to protect the head from flies, both real and artificial. A hood is obviously essential because on really wet days, it stops the water from trickling down the back of the neck. If you decide on a hat, then there are some really fancy ones on the market. A waterproof sou'wester is good as it comes with a downturned brim so the water doesn't collect up on top, but there are dozens of other styles and fabrics, so there's plenty of choice.

I must say that as a family we must look a pretty odd lot when we go out fishing. There's Rod and his father in their peaked wool country caps and Rod's mother in her black and white plastic sou'wester. Sister-in-law Lesley, who looks as if she's just stepped from the front cover of Vogue, her husband Fred in something equally stylish and me, either in my battered felt cap or my Russian bonnet which practically covers everything apart from eyes and nose!

There's nothing like a warm head, especially if you really suffer in the cold like I do. Even if I'm warmed from within with a steaming bowl of porridge for breakfast, or a nip of whisky at lunchtime, five minutes in a biting wind and all my extremities go numb. If it's frosty, out comes the woollen cowl, which looks like a huge knitted Balaclava and leaves me looking and feeling like an SAS member on a survival course. So if you're like me, maybe you'll consider a hat with earflaps which ties under the chin, can't blow off in a gale and will also protect the sides of the face from wind and airborne flies. (Anyone who's caught the back of a head or clipped an ear with a three-pronged salmon hook will appreciate the advantages of that!)

A note here for the fussy fisher: if you have to get to the office later on, a hat will keep you warm and dry and it will also protect your nicely permed hair. Or at least, it is supposed to protect your hair! I recall one occasion when I'd snatched a few early morning hours by the river before returning to London to read the evening news. Well, it had been an unusually smooth bulletin with no last-minute panics or disasters and I was just congratulating myself on being able to mix business with pleasure on a work day when a rather bemused news editor came over to my desk. 'I've just had a lady viewer on the phone,' he said, '...says she enjoys watching you on the news, but can't understand why you have to wear a wig, and why on earth can't you get a decent one! I assured her that our newscasters do not wear wigs, but she says she's a hairdresser and she knows a wig when she sees one!' So much for mixing business and pleasure, and so much for all the backcombing and hairspray I'd piled on to hide the traces of my morning trip to the river!

Onto footwear, something the TV viewers aren't particularly concerned with, since it's usually not on show. Here the angler needs something that's comfortable, robust and waterproof. Again, like the jacket, what he chooses depends on where he plans to fish. If it's just from the bank, then wellies will do fine, but I have to say that I've never met a salmon fisher who doesn't step out into the water at some stage. You may be different, but I very much doubt it, so I would suggest that you'll almost certainly need to invest in a good pair of waders. These are basically extended wellies and there are two different sorts with very original names — those which come up to the thighs are thigh waders, and those that reach over the chest are chest waders. Thigh waders are held up with strips of rubber which attach to a belt or trousers whereas chest waders usually have extendable straps which loop over the shoulder and clip back onto the front — a bit like salopettes in skiing. For safety's sake, in providing a grip on slippery stones and the like you should buy waders with felt or studded soles.

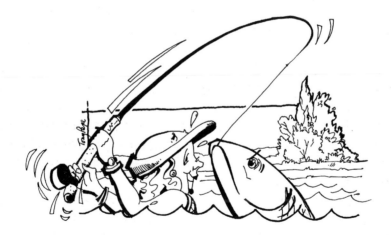

When I first started fishing I bought myself a pair of thigh waders, simply because I thought they looked more elegant. They were easy to walk in and they were fine when the weather was warm and the water was low. But as my fishing progressed and I began to fish in worse weather and deeper pools I realised that a rethink was needed. The final straw came when I hooked a small salmon locally and started to follow it downstream. It wasn't a big one, but it was spring and the fish was a real livewire, pulling the rod this way and that, and yanking off great handfuls of line. I seemed to be doing quite well in trying to control it, until it dawned on me that I was getting in deeper and deeper, with the water inching ever higher up my thighs to the tops of my waders. Of course, in the panic to stay dry, I lost both my concentration and the fish and got a good soaking into the bargain. Now there's nothing worse than clammy feet inside sopping waders, so after that I went out and bought a pair of chest waders and I'm now a convert. As well as keeping feet dry, the other advantage is that they're much warmer and they really do protect your back from the wind. They also allow you to sit down comfortably on the river bank without getting a wet bottom, and that's useful if you're having lunch by the river or simply taking a breather.

There are some disadvantages to chest waders though, for they can get extremely hot and sticky in summer and they're not the easiest things to walk about in, especially if it's a long trek from car to river. They can also be devilishly difficult to put on and take off; I still haven't quite mastered the knack and usually have to prop myself up against the car or a nearby hedge, or get someone to steady me whilst I struggle in and out of them. Most important of all, should you fall into the water they're probably not the safest things to be wearing. Another minor drawback, if

Eight months' pregnant and still fishing with my mother-in-law, Pat, on the Eden

you're worried about style, is that they often look so incredibly bulky, especially with jumpers and even jackets pushed down inside. But then fishing isn't about fashion, so don't let your appearance get you down. One other thought on chest waders; they're not that good for expectant ladies! Eight months pregnant and still wanting to fish, I struggled to pull them over the bump and had to resort to my wellies. Maternity waders? Now there's a thought! I wonder if they'd ever catch on?

As for price, again, waders don't come cheap and you'll be very lucky to get change from £50 for an average pair, but I personally think this is one area where it's worth paying that little bit extra. After all, you don't want to end up with something badly made that will leak at the seams after a few months. You also don't want something that's going to pinch your feet, so when I bought, I went up at least half a shoe size. Feet encased in rubber are guaranteed to sweat and expand and in cold weather, you'll need to leave plenty of room for all those woolly socks.

Finally, you might like to try a pair of neoprenes and these are catching on fast although I have to say, it takes a brave man or woman to wear them. These are basically dry-suits which fit reasonably snugly against the body but don't leave a lot to the imagination! In other words, you either have to be pretty trim or just an extrovert to wear them! They're quite pricey but they do keep a body warm and dry and they're not nearly as cumbersome as the regular waders. The only person I know with a pair is our friend Mike Bullough and he swears by them, but then he's pretty trim. I'm not sure I could be so confident!

I know that I keep harping back to this, but on cold days, warmth is crucial when fishing, so another must is a pair of gloves. Like my head and face, my hands suffer terribly when I'm outside, so I've bought several pairs of thermal gloves which are nice and warm but not too thick that I can't tie and untie knots or feel the line. I've also lost several pairs of gloves on these little river trips and if anyone knows a better way of not losing them than the old-fashioned way of sewing them to a length of elastic and then feeding it down through my coat sleeves, please let me know!

But if you find that gloves cramp your casting, then a good compromise may be a pair of mittens which are cut off at the finger joints but keep palms warm and leave fingers free for angling matters. Whatever you decide on though, take along a spare pair because it's surprising how soon they become waterlogged.

Although it's no fun fishing with cold, wet hands some people find ingenious ways of keeping themselves warm and dry. One of the best I've seen is the wearing of rubber washing-up gloves over woollen ones. (Please note, it took a woman to come up with this idea. Kitchen glove manufacturers, also note, if this is a trend which is to catch on, can we please have less garish colours. Shocking pink or bright yellow really does tend to jar amongst all that green!)

Finally, on the subject of hands, if you really suffer from chilblains, you might want to try a small hand-warmer, which is a special gadget that fits in the pocket and dissipates heat when held. I can't recommend these personally since I've yet to try one, but I hear they're taken on Arctic expeditions, so they must be reasonably good! Some have to be prepared prior to the off by popping them into boiling water so that they can store the energy they will later release as heat.

Onto necks, and a scarf can be another welcome addition to the fishing wardrobe and, if it's big enough, it can often double as a hat. Just be careful though that there aren't bits of material flapping about which might get in the way of the rod and the reel, or it could all end in disaster. As a beginner you'll have enough knots in your line without having to battle with more round your neck!

If scarves are useful, then thermal underwear is an absolute must. Years on the road as a radio and TV reporter has convinced me of that. Memories of cold, long assignments still come back to haunt me; long, freezing nights spent with the ladies of Greenham Common, (remem-

When all you're catching is a cold...

ber the early eighties and cruise missiles?), that mammoth charity walk by the England cricket captain in the depths of a northern winter. Ian Botham was my hero, and he'd been on the road for weeks, covering hundreds of miles to raise money for charity. I was sent to cover the story for Border TV and I breathlessly caught up with him as he limped over the top of a very snowy and frosty Shap Fell. Understandably at the time, he seemed rather wary of reporters, so he wasn't that forthcoming, but I pressed on and he was polite and courteous. I think the

River Cassley ghillie Jim Renwick with the sort of fish you long to catch

Safely-landed, a 7lb spring Dee salmon

final straw came when I asked the daftest question, 'What part of your body hurts the most on this walk?' You can guess what his reply was.

Always wear more pairs of woolly socks than you think you'll need. These are vital and if they're thermal, even better. I learned the hard way many years ago on a freezing cold day in Manchester, that feet encased in rubber can become unbearably cold! Again, I wasn't fishing but filming for the BBC. It had been snowing hard as it is wont to do in Manchester and I was just congratulating myself on being in a nice, warm office when I was told to take a camera crew and go and interview a union leader about the miners' strike. We duly rooted out the office wellies, (two sizes too big, of course) but, being totally unprepared, I had no socks, just the nylons I stood up in. 'Don't bother me with trivialities,' said the no-nonsense news editor, 'just go and get the story!' Well, after 20 minutes of standing in a foot of snow outside our victim's house I was really suffering. The sheer stockings were proving sheer murder as the cold seeped through the rubber boots. Half-an-hour on, I couldn't feel my toes. Ten minutes later, and I could hardly stand with the pain, and it was only when the cameraman, a real gentleman, offered me his gloves as makeshift socks that I was able to continue the job without too many complaints. Needless to say, the union

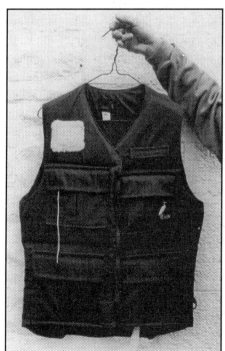

The indispensable life-jacket

man had inconveniently slipped out the back door, so we had waited in vain! But I've always remembered that day and the nightmare of frozen feet, and now I'm prepared for the worst with thermal socks and fleecy insoles.

You may find that on freezing days, keeping warm can become an angler's obsession and the best advice I can give is always to take along more layers than you think you'll need. Things can always be removed, but it's not so easy to warm up if you've only the got the one jumper.

What about colour? True, a lot of fishing clothes seem to be green, and personally, I do think it's correct to wear something that blends in with nature, but really, it doesn't matter. I don't think there's any firm evidence that wearing a shocking pink jacket will actually frighten the fish, you'll probably be more likely to frighten the farm animals.

Finally, let me mention two items which also feature in the chapter on safety, but which are rather important for your fishing wardrobe. The first is an angling life jacket and these are rather expensive, but they're also quite smart and they will keep you warm. Obviously, if you do have the misfortune to fall into some deep water, they could just save your life.

The second item is a pair of glasses or sunglasses. Now, good fun can be had with a pair of polarised sunglasses because you'll find they help you to see under the water to find out where the fish are lying, but the main reason I wear them is, again, one of safety. Proper safety glasses with wrap-around side lenses are particularly good items which will not detract from your vision. Horrible accidents can happen in fishing and hooks can end up embedded anywhere, so don't devalue your sight and make sure you protect your eyes.

Putting it all together

Tis an affair of luck.

Henry Van Dyke, Fisherman's Luck

When I first started fishing for salmon, I came to the conclusion that angling was all about luck. That's because, apart from the very first time, (beginner's luck, which everyone is entitled to, surely?) I never seemed to catch very much. Oh, it wasn't through want of trying. Sometimes I would flog away for hours on end, returning home tired and dispirited, especially after watching other, more fortunate anglers pulling out fish left, right and centre. I concluded that I just wasn't a lucky person.

Take my track-record in competitions for instance. Now, I've always been a sucker for games and gambles and throughout my life I've bought literally thousands and thousands of raffle and tombola tickets. All without success I hasten to add. Indeed, the only thing I've ever won was something I'd rather have done without. It was a gallon of motor-oil! I won it at a rather fancy media ball at one of London's smartest Hyde Park hotels. They called out my ticket number and dressed to kill and filled with expectation, I climbed the steps to the stage of the ballroom to claim my unknown prize, then rather red-faced, staggered back down again hauling this large can of lubricant with me. I have to confess that rather than having to make a less than grand exit with a greasy can, I abandoned it under a table and fled empty-handed!

Maybe I should have kept it. It might have come in useful for oiling rusty reels, because as I progressed in my fishing and began to land more fish, I realised that although luck can play a great part in catching salmon, if you find you're not getting them, there's often another reason. It could be that you're not using the right tackle, or you've not gauged the right weather conditions, or you're just not good enough!

Don't despair though. A beginner may not have the necessary skills to guarantee a fish, but he can still give himself a sporting chance by making sure that the equipment he's using is in good working order and is properly assembled. As everybody knows, if you want a job doing properly, you've got to do it yourself, therefore a trainee fisher should start as he means to go on and learn to tackle up himself. It might not always be necessary, especially if you've got a ghillie on the beat, but if you can take responsibility for your own rod, reel and line, there will be no-one else to blame if something goes wrong; a philosophy which will stand you in good stead and keep you on good terms with other fishing friends. Anglers have long memories and I've never forgotten losing a salmon when a fly which hadn't been tied on properly slipped off the leader. Of course, I'd asked somebody else (no names mentioned!) to put it on for me. I can never look at that person now without seeing a large salmon disappearing into the distance.

Another reason for becoming self-sufficient is that although it may be a struggle at first, it's so much more satisfying to master the technicalities. Once you know the equipment and how it slots together and comes apart, trips to the river will be more enjoyable, and you'll be a confident fisher. I must admit that as a beginner, the temptation is to let the experienced fisher take charge and I did spend my first year expecting whoever had taken me fishing to sort out whatever problems arose. 'Oh, I don't know what's happened. My fly just seems to have disappeared. Do you think you could tie on another...?' 'Oh, I seem to have got my line all twisted, do you think you could possibly help?'

Such requests are generally received with quite good humour. It's only when they become a little more involved that you may come up against a brick wall. Don't expect a stampede if you end up saying 'Look, I've got this favourite fly and when I cast back, it got tangled up in that tree. Do you think you could do me a favour and shin up there and try to get it down?'

And as you go on, you'll realise that although fishing is a companionable sort of sport, it can also be a solitary one. Sometimes a group of anglers will be casting fairly closely together, which means it's easy to ask for help. More often than not, though, the fisher will find himself a quarter of a mile or more downstream from the nearest rod. It's then that you will really start to iron out your own problems.

I must say, I've never regretted becoming an independent fisher. It means if I wake up in the morning and decide to go to the river, I'm not at the mercy of husband, father, ghillie, the milkman, or whoever, when it comes to tackling up. I may not be an expert fisher, but I can still understand my own equipment and do my own thing. You should be able to as well. Let's face it, you may be the best beginner in the world, but people do get tired of being asked to change flies, tie knots and generally nanny the novice, and who can blame them?

Fishers are generally accommodating people who will willingly give help and advice to others, but, at the end of the day, unless they're being paid specifically to look after you, (i.e. to ghillie for you) or are quite doting (and even this can become strained), there will come a stage when they too will want to fish rather than fuss. At the very least, they'll want to see some sort of effort. That is, that you are also prepared to have a go at wading into the rough water to rescue a sunken fly caught on a rock, or crawling into the prickly gorse bush to untangle the line.

Incidentally, if you really get into desperate trouble and simply can't sort it out yourself, always go for the most mature fisher! Now this riverside veteran should have a wealth of local knowledge and patience. He's usually seen and done it all before and will be delighted to pass on a few old timer's tips. As a beginner, the one to avoid is the younger, more aggressive angler, because he's there for two reasons only: to demonstrate his prowess on the water and to catch fish. So, unless you're a film star lookalike or he's very much in debt to you because you're paying for his day's sport, he won't feel the slightest urge to come to the rescue and will be generally unamused by requests for help.

So let's put it all together and tackle-up! Let's start with the rod. Fly-rods are so long and unwieldy, fishers generally assemble them when they arrive at the river, unless you've got a rod-carrier on top of your car (or a stretch limo!). However, as a beginner, it won't do any harm to have a practice run before you set off for the water and it might save a lot of potential embarrassment in front of other fishers! If the weather's fine, the garden is as good a place as any to have a go, especially if you've got a large lawn, free from overhanging trees or wires. Take the rod from its sleeve. It will usually be in three parts and what you must do is to slot the joints, or ferrules firmly together, thin ends pushing into thicker ends. Now you should have something which tapers from end to tip. Take a good look at it. There's a thickish handle at one end, which is called the butt and this is often encased in a firm cork covering or some non-slip material. In the middle of the butt there's the reel-seat, and this can be made out of plastic or metal and it's where the reel sits when it's screwed into place. At intervals dotted along the underside of the rod are small, round rings, through which the line is threaded. These get smaller as the rod narrows, with the final ring at the rod-point, which is sometimes called the tip-ring. The only other thing of note on the rod is a tiny loop of wire, which is found just above the butt, and this is often used as an anchor for the fly when the rod is being carried. Now, check that the rod-rings are aligned. Waggle the rod about a bit, taking care not to hit anything. It should feel firm but flexible. The ferrules on a new rod should be nice and stiff, but they will soon loosen with use age and this can occasionally have catastrophic results.

My husband tells the story of how on a boiling hot July day, he and his cousin Robbie staggered four miles in waders up a hillside to a place called Loch Dubh in Argyllshire. There would, no doubt have been much huffing and puffing, but the thought of all those Highland fish was enough to spur them on. Two hours later, they were enjoying a couple of cold beers drinking in the view of the mountain tops, having congratulated themselves on making the effort to get up there. Unhappily though, on Robbie's first cast his rod broke in two. He hadn't tightened the joints properly and could only watch in horror as the top half of his rod flew off, broke his leader and went sailing into the distance. Loch Dubh, which in Gaelic means the Black Loch, was living up to its name!

Of course, the lads thought they must be jinxed, but again, preparation is all and I am told that this sort of disaster can often be prevented by rubbing the rod-joints with a piece of candlewax before slotting them together. The theory is that the wax acts as a seal and helps to stop any loosening, although I've noticed that some anglers make extra sure that the rod stays together by sticking insulating tape over the joints. With all these precautions, don't be surprised if it's incredibly difficult to take the rod to bits again. I once watched a party of fishers trying to dismantle one and it was quite hilarious. Half a dozen or so of them all huffing and puffing and pulling in different directions as they tried to prize the rod apart. It was just like a tug-o'-war match and it can't have done the poor old rod much good! What they should have done, older and wiser fishers tell me, is to don a pair of rubber gloves and twist the offending portions apart. It apparently never fails!

There, your rod is up, and you can be proud of yourself. Now lean it somewhere safe, where it isn't going to fall or knock against anything and turn your attention to your reel.

As we already know from the chapter on tackle, a reel needs backing, line and leader. Backing is wound on first, followed by line, but joining these two together is a fiddly business and, although I said that you must learn to do everything yourself, this is one task that I don't really recommend for a beginner. Having watched my husband painstakingly splicing the two together, I reckon it's a job only for the experienced.

My advice is to buy a length of line which is already attached to the backing or, failing that, ask the assistant in the tackle shop to join the two together for you. You'll find that the people in sporting shops, like ghillies, are well used to being asked such things. Indeed, they often have small machines behind the counter, which will do in ten minutes what could take you or me the better part of a day. Of course, if they do

Mounting the reel on the rod

it, you can hopefully fish with confidence, knowing that it's all perfect with backing and line correctly spliced together and properly mounted on the reel.

The next step is to attach the reel to the rod. If you look in the middle of the rod-butt, you'll find the metal or plastic reel-holder and what you want to do is slot the bar of the reel into the bottom ring of the housing. Now, press the reel against the rod and put the top ring of the reel holder over the upper part of the bar and screw it firmly into place. The reel should now be sitting securely on the rod. Make sure that you get the reel the right way round, though. That is, placed to suit the hand you wish to reel in with. A right-handed fisher would usually have the handle on the right side. Someone left-handed, or who prefers to reel in with the left hand, will presumably want it sitting the other way. Also note that line and backing should be wound on according to whether you're right or left-handed, so tell your tackle-shop assistant before the start of the job what your preference is.

Again, it really is worth making sure that the reel is secure on the rod; a friend of ours tells a hilarious tale about how he was fishing beautifully on a Welsh river when all of a sudden, he hooked a heavy fish and in all the energetic playing of it, the reel worked itself loose and fell away from the rod onto the grass. Now, it would take a very clever person to put a reel back on a rod while still playing a fish. Indeed, when you think of it, those precious few seconds of lost concentration might make all the difference between letting a fish go and keeping it. Luckily though, he wasn't alone and his teenage son calmly picked up the reel and continued to play the fish. So, with father clutching the rod, and son working the reel, they eventually landed the salmon!

Now, if that happened to you as a beginner, you'd be in big trouble, so go back to your rod and double-check that

A rod ring, this is the largest one nearest to the butt-end

the reel is tightly screwed onto the rod. Now you must draw some line off the reel. It needs to come off in a straight line and do take care that it isn't bent round one of the bars or guides across the reel, otherwise you won't be able to cast properly . Next thread the line through the rod-rings, but again be very careful not to miss one out because it's something that's easily done, and it'll drive you mad when you find that everything's set up, but the line is jerking through the rod on each cast because you've missed a ring. Having threaded it through, pull out a couple of metres or so and either lie the rod down or lean it in a safe place where it won't fall over.

Your line is now ready for its nylon, or leader as we shall call it, though it's also referred to as a cast. As I mentioned earlier, leaders can be bought already made up, but I prefer to get a spool of nylon and make my own. It's much cheaper and it's quite easy and honestly, if I can do it, anyone can. Let's assume you are making your own. Take the spool of nylon and cut off a length. A very rough guide is two arm-spans, but what you basically want is something that's three-quarters the length of the rod; always overestimate rather than underestimate.

The length of nylon depends on the length of rod; obviously, a longer rod will need more leader and a smaller one, appreciably less. And of course, like everything else in angling, it all seems to depend on when and where you're fishing. For example, some fishers prefer to use a shorter length of leader in the spring and a longer length in the summer. If in doubt, consult the experts!

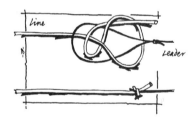

Figure of eight knot for joining leader to line

To join leader to line, take the nylon and make a loop in the end. Then, take the line and secure it through the loop, with a figure-of-eight knot. This is actually one knot which it took me ages to master, especially being short-sighted. In fact I got to the stage where I could barely see where the nylon was going. I'd just about given up on the job when my husband brought two lengths of rope into the kitchen and told me to practice on those — it worked! In big scale, I could see how it all fitted together and half-an-hour later, I had it cracked.

Now, we're on the last lap and the final thing to do is to tie the fly to the end of the leader. You'll find there are many different sort of knots in fishing and as you progress, you'll try many before settling on the one that suits you best. So I'll give you just the one, which I use practically all the time and which has been quite effective. It's known as the half-blood or clinch knot and it goes as follows. Put the nylon through the eye of the fly, twist it round half-a-dozen times or so, and then push it back through itself. Some folk prefer to push the nylon back through the eye of the fly and then through the loop which means the end of the nylon lies flat and doesn't stick out.

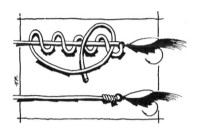

Clinch knot for tying fly to leader

Some others are not quite so scientific and when they've twisted the nylon, they spit on it to wet it. This is what's known in the trade as greasing or moistening the nylon and it helps to reduce friction and heat which means the knot is less likely to slip or snap when a fish is on and everything is straining.

You may now be despairing, especially if, like me, you're not technical, but please don't. The thing is, if you want to become a fisher, you must learn to tie certain basic knots, and tie them securely. Though having said that, there can't be an angler alive who hasn't at some stage doubted his own handiwork. It seems to me that no matter how many salmon I catch, when the moment of truth comes, there's always that tiny, niggling thought. 'Was the fly tied on tightly enough? Will it hold, or will the knot slowly slip?!' Well, I'm learning through practice, experience and unfortunately through a few lost fish. I hope you have better luck!

So, the fly is on and now it must be pulled tightly to make sure everything is secure. But don't use fingers, because that's a sure way to a nasty accident. Instead, take a pair of scissors, grip the closed blades, place one of the finger grips in the bend of the hook and pull the leader with the other hand. This will test whether it's going to hold, and it'll also reduce the chance of pulling the hook into your hand. Then once it's tight, you can clip the hook to one of the bars on the reel. Some people use the small ring just above the butt and as I said earlier, this is actually designed as a fly-holder, but I've learned to my cost to avoid this 'useful' little gadget, because the rod is carried by the butt and if it's a big fly, with big hooks, the chances of catching yourself are fairly high.

So there you are, all tackled up and ready to go! Remember though that you will often be fishing a long way from home, so before setting off, it's worth making a thorough check that you have everything you need. Beginners are enthusiastic and eager to get started and that's good, but there's nothing worse than getting to the water and finding out with anguish that you've left a vital piece of equipment in the cupboard at home.

To prevent this, make a list and tick things off. Rod, reel with backing and line, spare reel, spare nylon, flies, hooks and scissors. You won't need that much, for unlike spinning or coarse fishing where the angler has to go armed to the teeth with all sorts of weights and baits, fly-fishing is really quite economical on tackle. I sometimes think it's like the difference between working in radio and working in television. In radio, I would set off to cover the story with a small tape recorder and a microphone and all I had to worry about was whether the thing was switched on and whether I'd got the levels right. Mind you, it did help to have some tape in the machine!

I recall one occasion, getting an exclusive interview with a famous boxer who was visiting the area. Well, knowing nothing about boxing, I researched the subject with great care and met my interviewee with fear and trepidation. However, he was a lovely, gentle giant of a man and we got on famously, so the scoop was there and all I had to do was to return to the station and edit the thing together. 'I've got your lead feature tonight', I called out cheerfully to the news editor who was working away on that evening's programme.

Or I might have had; I can still remember it now, opening up the tape recorder and gazing in horror at the empty space!

Finally it's as well to say that there are many different schools of thought about how lines, casts and flies should be tied. All I've given you is a simple selection, because, as far as I'm concerned, simplicity is the key to fishing. As I've already confessed, I find anything remotely technical impossible to handle, so in my early angling days, I decided to adopt the KISS philosophy, which is a method taught to all trainee journalists who are learning to write news stories, and one I've always thought was eminently sensible. K.I.S.S. — Keep It Simple Stupid. Those who wish to know more about the finer points of knots and lines should consult a far more expert book than this or, alternatively, a sailor!

Casting

If your line's not in the water, you'll not catch fish

My father-in-law

By now, you may have a beginner's idea as to how the tackle is put together and the next bit of the operation is to try it out and, although the first trip to the water can be daunting, don't worry. Unless you fall out with your fishing companions, fall into the river, or onto a sharp hook, it promises to be a wonderful day, so enjoy it!

Hopefully, you've arrived at a pleasant, quiet part of the water, perhaps with an experienced angler by your side. Take the rod out of its sleeve, assemble it and attach the reel. Thread the line through the rod-rings, but don't attach leader and fly just yet. These can wait until you're more confident. Now you are ready for your first casting lesson.

Casting is an art...

Casting is a thing which looks very simple when you watch someone else doing it, but the reality is rather different. Some people pick it up very quickly, but I'm afraid that I'm one of those who's still serving several years of a long and frustrating apprenticeship before getting it anywhere near right. Casting is also difficult to describe in words and the only way you will really learn is by being taught beside the water by an expert. Bear with me, though, and remember, this is just a simple guide which will give the bare bones of the operation.

Basically, the aim in fly-fishing is to project the fly at the end of your nylon, or leader, out into the river. It should usually go across and downstream in order to cover as much water as possible, but like everything else in fishing, there are exceptions to this rule, such as when the river is too narrow to cast across. You generally fish your way downstream, starting at the head of the pool, though there are exceptions to this rule too, which you'll discover as you progress.

There are some would-be anglers, of course, who ignore all the rules and just do their own thing like our friend Bill, who'd never fished in his life until he was taken by my father-in-law to a lovely stretch of water on the River Don in Aberdeenshire. Bill was shown how and where to put his fly, but he obviously had very little sense of direction as he soon started casting upstream, downstream, in fact all over the stream. 'Never mind', thought Tommy. 'He looks happy enough, I'll let him get on with it.' And off he went to fish himself. The next thing he knew, there were sounds of panic coming from up the riverbank. 'The silly bugger's fallen in!' thought Tommy, hearing the frantic screams, so he downed rod and raced back to the spot where he'd left Bill. And there he was, certainly in trouble, but the sort of trouble any angler would love to find himself in — facing upstream, rod bent double, with a large salmon, 20 pounds at the very least, splashing about on the end! A little unconventional, I know, but that's fishing. Don't however be tempted to follow this lead. Bill himself agreed that it must have been luck and, unless told differently by an expert or a ghillie, as a beginner, you will fish downstream.

As the current brings the fly round in an arc on the water, I've been told the object is to make it swim in a lifelike and attractive way trying to imitate one of the salmon's favourite foods. That's my theory anyhow, despite the fact that we've already established that salmon don't feed in freshwater. Whatever we're trying to imitate, though, it must look lifelike and attractive and, depending on the time of year, this can either be a small fish, a waterborne insect, or plankton. Your fly is therefore the sprat to catch the mackerel. Your rod is a means of projecting both line and fly out and across the water. This action is called casting.

So, to the technicalities and there are different ways of casting, but the one I was taught which seems to be widely and popularly used is the standard overhead cast. Stand comfortably with feet apart; it's important to be well balanced as you don't want to end up falling over after an over-energetic throw, do you? If you're right-handed, hold the rod with the right hand near the top of the cork grip, with the left hand positioned a few inches down from the reel. Now pull out a few metres of line and get the feel of the rod by lifting the line off the ground and throwing it out and back behind you. Once you've got used to that, you can start to pause momentarily on the back cast, before trying to arc the rod crisply forward.

This is not as easy as it seems and I remember wrapping the line round my neck a few times before I gradually got into the swing of things. I soon learnt too that the length of pause as you cast back is terribly important, but if it's any help, I was told to take the line back and then count, 'one-two', before bringing it forward again. I was also told that all these movements, forward and back, must be firm and decisive, otherwise the line just won't flow.

You should now be able to throw the line some distance, the next step is to learn to shoot it. To do this, I pull off an extra couple of metres of line or so and let it lie at the ground by my feet. Next, with the fore-finger of my right hand, I hold the line against the rod at the top of the butt. Then, keeping hold of the line as I cast back, I pause, then I flick the rod forward and let go of the line. It generally comes shooting through the rod-rings, but as we all know, theory is one thing, practice is quite another.

Casting over the head of the run on the Cassley. Seamus, the ghillie in attendance

Shooting line is probably the most difficult action of all for any beginner to master, because it's critical at what time you release the line. Many people become very frustrated in trying to master the technique; I for one, almost gave up the whole job, becoming so infuriated by letting go at the wrong time. Basically casting is all down to timing, and it can be highly frustrating trying to get it right, but it's a comfort to know that it's rather like learning to strike a golf ball or ride a bike, once it's timed correctly, everything gradually begins to fall into place, hopefully the right place! Don't get too confident though. You'll see some experts by the river shooting metres and metres and making it look as easy as pie. As a beginner don't be tempted to try to copy this, or to take things too quickly — you'll get into an awful mess with spare line going here, there and everywhere. Wait until you can shoot a couple of metres before you try another, and so on. For, as you'll discover, in casting, there are a host of other things which can go wrong. I'll list just a few of the ones that bedevil me.

Taking the rod back too far is a common problem with a beginner. I was told that the rod should stop at the ear of the casting shoulder and taking it any further may mean that the line hits the ground behind, which would almost certainly mar the cast, or worse still, break the fly on a stone or rock.

Looking backwards instead of forwards when casting back. The line is meant to curl round in a loop before it's brought forward again and I used to reassure myself by glancing over my shoulder to make sure this was happening. I've learnt not to do it, because it simply puts me off balance and mars the forward cast.

Timing is crucial; the duration of the pause on the back cast is vital and if the line cracks like the sound of a whip when you bring it forward, it may not have had enough time to straighten out behind. The sound you want to hear when you cast out is a low satisfying whistle as the line is pulled smoothly and quickly from your hand and through the rings of the rod.

Wind knots really are the scourge of the beginner, for as the line flails about, as it surely will in the early days, you may find that the nylon twists and that tiny knots appear. These must be taken out immediately, as they weaken the nylon and can cause it to snap, which is one thing if you don't mind losing a fly, but quite another when it comes to sacrificing a fish! I was with a friend who hooked a fair-sized salmon and was just about to bring it to the net when the line went slack and the fish was gone. In anguish, she looked down at what was left of the leader which had snapped just below a tiny knot. 'Your own fault', said her husband, rather unkindly. I tell you, fishing can lead to all sorts of arguments! Wind knots are generally quite impossible to undo, by the way, and it's often simpler to abandon the existing leader and put on a new piece of nylon, but if you don't like waste, a tip learned from an old ghillie is to use the sharp point of a safety pin or the tip of a fly-hook to try to untangle the mess.

Trying too hard. Casting is a deliberate and rhythmical action, but if too much force is used, it often defeats the purpose and prevents the rod from being given enough time to do its job. I had some hilarious hours in the early days, when I would be red-faced and bent double trying to hurl the line into the water. I remember, on one famous occasion, Neil Graesser giving me some much appreciated lessons, as he tried not to laugh. 'Relax! Stand up straight! You look like you're trying to throw yourself in the water, never mind the fly', he said at the end of the first day. I went away with the advice: 'Let the rod do the work! You are there simply to guide it. Patience is the word, patience and timing.'

Now, if you're right-handed, you'll most probably have been casting over your right shoulder. But sooner or later, you'll find yourself trying to avoid bushes or overhanging trees, or even the angle of the wind, and then you'll see that it's worth learning to be ambidextrous or even to back cast over your left shoulder. This action feels most peculiar at first, rather like trying to write with the wrong hand. However it's worth persevering with as it'll sometimes mean the difference between being able to fish or not. Indeed, two of the biggest headaches for the beginner when he's casting are the trees and bank behind him and the wind. Their combined effects can be devastating.

Just imagine the scene: a wonderful pool, where you've seen fish jumping, so you know they're there, the water conditions are right for taking, fellow fishers are optimistic and you're just in the mood to catch a big one! The problem is though, there's a fierce wind blowing and each time you try to cast back, your line is being blown prematurely forwards, creating a real mess. Then the wind direction changes and the line starts flying round your neck and ears. You try to shift position, but it's still causing all sorts of misery, as the fly is blown in and out of gorse bushes and tree branches! Despite the show of fish, the fair-weather angler or fainthearted beginner gives up and goes home, resolving to return only when the weather improves. The more determined, some would say foolish, among us hang in there and look for an alternative cast. When I first started fishing, I was told that the roll or Spey cast was a rather difficult movement, a sort of stage two, which was to be learnt only when I'd mastered stage one, that is, the standard overhead cast. However, having talked to various fishers, it seems the Spey cast is very much in vogue these days. Indeed the eminent fisher and writer, Hugh

Falkus, recommends it to all his beginners. In his words: 'It is a waste to equip yourself with expensive tackle and rent a costly beat, if you haven't the technique to take advantage of it. An ability to switch cast — that is to make roll, single-Spey and double-Spey casts — is essential to every salmon fisherman.'

Put very simply, Spey casting involves bringing the line towards you and then rolling it energetically forwards again. The theory is that, unlike the standard overhead cast, it prevents the fly from getting hooked up in anything as it should never really pass behind you and thus, you can always see what it's doing. I've had a tentative go at Spey-casting and, I must admit, I find it quite difficult, but that's probably because I'm so used to the overhead cast. However, I'm determined to persevere and have promised myself lessons, so we'll see how we get on!

Whichever cast you're learning, there's no substitute for practice. Of course some beginners pick up the skill very quickly and there are others (myself included) who take several years to come anywhere near to perfection, so if you have problems too, don't worry about it. You don't have to be a superb fly-caster to catch a fish. My own record has certainly proved that, so don't be disheartened. What really matters is the enthusiasm and the dedication. It is immensely satisfying to be able to throw a good line, so keep plugging away.

Now you have a vague idea of casting and the next step is to learn what to do with the fly, that is, how to control it as it crosses the water.If you've been practising without a fly, now might be a good time to put one on and don't forget the leader, will you?

How the fly is worked in the water is really a matter for the individual. Some fishers let nature take its course, casting out and letting the fly drift and the water current move it around. But I tend to think that nature sometimes needs a little bit of help and I like to take an active part in the proceedings. As I've already said, what we're trying to do in fly-fishing is to imitate something like a small fish, or an insect. When controlling the fly, therefore, the aim is to inject movement into it, to make it look appetizing and lifelike to the salmon. To do this and create the necessary actions to make it swim realistically, the fly can be pulled up against the current of water through which it is being drawn.

So, standing at an angle to the water, cast out. Your fly should land several feet in front and, as it swings round towards you, pull in a few inches of line. Pause, then pull in a few more inches. Vary the speed, sometimes fast, sometimes slow. It'll all give movement and life to the fly. This pulling of the line is called handlining. It keeps the line fairly taut, and this is very important when keeping in contact with the fly. If the line looks crooked on the water, you must straighten it out, or mend

Dad, Natasha and Mum, raring to go at the Dee hut. Below: Natasha, just six weeks old with fellow fishers at the Achness Hotel

Look at that grin! An 11lb salmon caught on the Cassley in May

The Cassley Falls, a great place to fish and watch the salmon leaping

Time to relax and talk flies with Neil Graesser OBE

it and this is done by flicking the rod-tip and sending the line out across the water. Once your fly has reached the near bank, that is, the bank nearest you, your cast is completed.

I've been told always to fish the line right round into the bank and to leave it there for a few seconds before continuing. Who knows, a fish may have followed the fly round and be studying it, or even be just about to take. Or there may be a fish lurking under the bank, again just waiting to bite, and too much haste may mean you miss out. However, if you wait and nothing happens, then you should be ready to cast again, but before you charge on, just wait a minute. You need to pull in several feet of line and you should also raise the rod slightly to lift the line off the water and let the water run off it. A shorter, lighter line is much easier to lift and the extra pause will give you time to compose yourself and may even give that elusive salmon a final chance to take. Of course, another reason for hesitating is that the fly may be stuck on something heavy in the water like a rock or a stone and by trying to force it out, you may not only mar the cast, but you could also break the rod.

There's a lot to take in there, but I leave you with one further thought. I've assumed that you have all this time been standing in one place. So this is as good a time as any to tell you that any fly-fisher worth his salt is a busy person and is frequently on the move! A couple of casts and he walks a few yards downstream. Two more casts and he moves again. Now this walking is called covering the water and, theoretically, it gives a better chance of putting the fly over a fish. The theory I imagine is that you look for him, rather than the other way round. It means that if the beat's a mile long, you'll be in for a lot of exercise, but that's just an added bonus!

Moving too slowly is a common fault for the beginner and I was as guilty as any in the early days. The result was that I would only cover a quarter of the water I should have done, and consequently, only caught a quarter of the fish. In fact I'm still regularly being told not to fish too long in one spot, especially if there's another angler coming up behind. I'm also told frequently never to obstruct another fisher or get too close to him, but as you become more confident, you'll find your own pace and be able to judge just how fast to go.

Sometimes, it may pay to fish a pool quickly and return later in the day, because flogging away at the same spot could mean that you end up irritating whatever's in there. At other times, if you see salmon, you may decide that it's worth returning to fish over them several times, while using a selection of different flies. These are all things that must be learned, usually by trial and error. Don't forget that variety is often the spice of life in angling, so if you've been at it for a while and nothing's happened, change the fly, or the angle of your cast, but above all, enjoy it!

There are two final thoughts on casting. It's worth checking the fly constantly, firstly to make sure that the hook isn't bent or broken and also that there's still one on! I once fished for a whole morning only to discover at lunchtime that I was fishing without a lure. Lord knows how I lost it; hopefully, it was later rather than earlier in the day.

And finally, if your fly gets stuck, either round a rock in the river, or up a tree, (as it most certainly will, at least 20 times a day!) remember that there are ways and means of getting out of the mess, but that the main thing is not to panic! In fishing, as in presenting, I always try to adopt the 'duck on water' philosophy. That is, no matter how fraught a bulletin threatens to become, you as the anchor, the person upfront, must always remain calm and unruffled. It's the vision of the duck gliding serenely along the water — underneath it may be paddling like mad to stay afloat!

Occasionally, though, panic does take over, as in the famous occasion when I couldn't make head nor tail of where I was in the programme and so I turned agitatedly to the camera and snapped, 'I'm sorry, I haven't a clue where we are.' Now, if I'd only done it with a smile, I'd have been alright, since I'm told that people aren't worried when things go wrong on TV, in fact they simply love it, just as long as you don't look worried or embarassed!

So too in fishing. Occasionally, panic will rule, but getting cross often makes matters worse; so, if you are in trouble with a stuck line, try the gentle approach first of all and waggle the rod-tip up and down. Obviously if that doesn't loosen things, then further drastic measures may be needed. But don't be tempted to use your rod to yank the line loose or it may break. Instead, put down the rod and give a sharp tug on the line. That probably won't work either and you'll still end up losing leader and fly, but at least you should recover the line.

There are other ways to get out of the mess; I once watched an old ghillie free a stuck line by almost karate-chopping the rod-butt with the side of his hand. I thought the thing would surely break in two, but instead, the rod just gave an almighty judder and the line slipped free. As a novice, please don't be tempted to try this; I don't want to be responsible for hundreds of broken rods! It is infuriating getting stuck, but don't be discouraged. I promise you, several trees will more than likely be scaled and dozens of river stones overturned before your first season is over — there's no way out. Lures will also be lost, so always take along an extra box of them; until you become a competent caster you'll certainly need them!

Catching, playing and landing a fish

Angling: incessant expectation, and perpetual disappointment.

Arthur Young, Travels in France

Y ou may be the best caster in the world by now, but if you want to catch something, you've got to use some cunning too! Just because there's some water about, doesn't mean there will automatically be anything in it.

In my few years on the river I've learnt that time and the elements conspire to thwart the salmon-fisher. Some rivers are better fished only at certain times of the season and that may only be for two or three months of the year and, of course, you, like me, will always turn up at the wrong place, on the wrong day! In other cases, weather conditions will be impossible and there won't be the slightest chance of tickling even a tadpole, let alone seeing a salmon. So before setting off, whether it's a local trip, or further afield, it's worth putting some effort into trying to find out if there's a reasonable chance of catching fish.

Some anglers are quite secretive about this sort of thing, hoping to keep the best beats for themselves, but most of us are a fairly generous lot, so do ask around. Particularly useful are the people in local tackle shops, who'll be able to disclose the numbers being caught in local rivers, on which beats and at what time of day. Yes, very often, time of day does matter!

Angling magazines too are mines of information when it comes to knowing how various rivers are faring. Some people check on the time of tides, the theory being that the fish come up with the fresh water and this can help if you're fishing a beat near an estuary, though I must say, in my experience it doesn't seem to make any difference what time the tide is as far as I'm concerned! If travelling away, ring up the local tackle shop or fishing hotel before you go. Sometimes they'll be quite honest and say, 'There's no water in the river, but rain is expected, so if you want to chance it and have a holiday, do come along.' Others will just want your custom and say 'Yes, it's OK'. Then, when you arrive, it'll often be a case of, 'You should have been here yesterday!'

I must admit that no matter how dedicated you are, there's nothing worse than fishing for days and having the feeling that there's nothing in the water. That said, there's no guarantee of catching anything even if you can see them. I remember one day on the Derwent in West Cumbria, when huge, silvery salmon were literally leaping round our feet. Did we catch anything? No, not one single fish!

However, let's assume that you've checked on the likelihood of there being something in the river. Now, when you get to the water, the next thing to remember is to go slowly and carefully. Salmon aren't as easily disturbed as some fish, like sea-trout for example, but you've still got to tread carefully if you want to succeed. I like this quote from a witty book lent to me by a colleague at work. It's called *Fly Fishing for Duffers*, (R.D. Peck, 1934), and it really does go back to basics! Mr Peck has a wonderful, dry sense of humour, which maybe he could afford in those wonderful fish-filled days of yesteryear and blunt comments like this are priceless! 'Your chance of a fish is much greater if he doesn't hear, (if fish do hear), see or feel you, your footfall, your rod, line, cast, flash, reflection or shadow.'

Always approach a pool with great care. It may be empty, true, but you don't want to risk scattering anything that is there by stamping or splashing about in waders. In the same vein, don't let dogs, children, grandma or whoever's with you bark, shout or generally make a disturbance on the bank, as vibrations can be easily transmitted. A friend of ours gets really mad if anyone slams a car door near the river and he's quite right too.

In the same vein, if fishing from a boat, try not to splash the oars, as this really sends the fish diving for cover. Watch the old timers, the ghillies and fishers of many years who do it with great nonchalance and dignity. Remember, you are the hunter, but the salmon has the upper hand, for he knows the nooks and crannies of his watery domain far better than any angler ever will.

So let's move on. From when to fish, to where to fish and this is a difficult area for a beginner to guide a beginner, but I'll try. A beat can be over a mile or more long, and that's an awful lot of water to cover when you're just taking pot luck! Where to cast your fly on such an expanse? I'm told that salmon can be found in almost any part of a river, but there are areas where you might just have a better chance of catching one.

For example, you'll often hear experienced anglers talking of a good pool, or a good lie and that's an area of the river where the fish does just that. Perhaps he wants a break from his run upstream and he's found a large rock to shelter against before moving on, or maybe there's a deep, cool pool to laze about in. Whatever the reason, a lie can certainly be one of the best spots to fish over, which is all very well, of course, if you happen to know where this fruitful place is. Another good area might be a streamy bit, for salmon are sometimes found in the rough water. The thing to remember is that if they're coming upstream, sooner or later they're bound to swim past your fly, so keep it wet and keep it moving, because no matter where the fish are, one thing's for sure: if your line's not in the water you'll not catch them.

The next thing to know is that, contrary to beginners' belief, salmon are found on both sides of the water! As a novice, it seemed to me that, the grass was literally always greener on the other side. Wherever we were, I was always being told to cast my fly over to the far bank because that's where the fish were. Well, that is often the case, but sometimes, just occasionally mind, the fish actually lie on your side, and then you don't have to try as hard.

This brings in the question of how far a fisher should wade across a river, especially if he only has fishing rights for one side of the bank. We rent a stretch of water where the fish definitely sit on our side and there's nothing more infuriating than to arrive to find that someone from the opposite bank has taken the liberty of wading right over, so that you find yourself fishing rod-tip to rod-tip. Personally, I think it's a case of being good-mannered and sensitive about the matter. I don't know whether it's the rule for all rivers, but two ghillies have advised me that it is alright to wade across, as long as you don't turn your back to the opposite bank.

Let's assume the scene is set; it's a good fishing day, slightly overcast, with a gentle breeze ruffling the water and you've found your good spot by the river and you've waded in. You cast back and the line shoots straight out in front of you. The red and black, medium-sized double you've so lovingly chosen goes swimming tantalisingly downstream, when suddenly, there's a sharp pull. A fish! Or is it?!

When I first started, people used to say, 'When you catch a salmon, there will be no doubt, you'll just know'. Well, I'm afraid I didn't just know. Left by my husband on one famous occasion on a local river, I hooked my fly on an underwater object and was convinced that I'd got something. The thing was, it just felt so realistic! Each time I wound in line, it would be taken out again, all the time moving and jerking about. I would have sworn there was a fish on the end, but I could not make any sense of it. In the end I accosted some walkers who happened to be passing by. 'Please, I've got this enormous fish on', I urged, 'and my husband is down the river — can you ask him to hurry up with the net?!' Fired by my enthusiasm, the walkers became runners as they set off at a hefty lick. Of course, when the net was brought, my face turned bright red as we landed a nice, fat branch. It just shows that unless you've caught a fish or two, it can be devilishly difficult to know and even now I still catch my fair share of rocks and branches and get over-excited, thinking it must be a salmon.

I'm not alone either, for even the experienced can get confused. My father-in-law confesses to once playing a hot-water bottle for what seemed like hours before he landed the wretched thing. Open-mouthed and bloated with water, I suppose it would seem quite fishlike as it slithered in and out of the streams!

Jaws — the big one!

Meanwhile, another chap we know hooked what he thought was a huge fish with great jaws, only to discover that what he'd been flirting with was a pair of false teeth fastened firmly to a small log!

But one of my favourite tales is the one about the Cumbrian doctor who was fishing the River Derwent when his rod nearly bent double.

He just couldn't get whatever was at the end of his line under control and the word went round the village that he must have on a whopping great salmon. The locals hadn't seen such excitement for many years and, one by one, they downed tools and made for the river to witness this exciting event. What a marathon! It took our hero three hours to bring his catch to the net and when he did, a huge cheer went up from the assembled crowd until they all realised what he'd been playing wasn't the salmon of the century, but an old tin bucket, weighted with cement!

So it's not that easy for beginners. Maybe for the experts — yes. But you and I can certainly be forgiven when it comes to the odd slip-up when hooking a salmon. After all, it depends on how the fish takes the fly as to what it feels like. For example, some of the more energetic types show no mercy and whack! your line is reeling violently and you're left struggling to control the rod. Other, more gentle types simply toy with the fly, gently tugging and sucking at it as they try to work out whether it's worth swallowing. Whatever happens, if there's movement at the end of the rod, there may be something there and if it really is a fish, it'll be the most exciting thing of all!

If you've something on the end, your rod-tip may start to judder and your line may begin to unwind from the reel as soon as you feel this initial pull. The temptation for the beginner must be to do something, at the very least to shout wildly for help, or to raise the rod, but this opens up a whole new debate. To strike at once, or to wait?

Now, I have found this to be a controversial field. My father-in-law, for example, is of the same school as the fishing expert Hugh Falkus and he'll tell you that you should always wait and give a salmon line, because by raising the rod and striking immediately, there's always the risk that you pull the fly straight out of the fish's mouth. It's far better, he says, to allow the fish to suck in the fly, then, as he turns and takes the line with him, the theory is that the barbs will be firmly pulled in and the fish will be well and truly hooked.

However, there's nothing like angling to divide a family and my husband takes the opposite view maintaining that a fisher should strike as soon as he feels a pull. This is also the view of Neil Graesser, who says the hook must be set before the fish has a chance to spit it out. Again, like anything in salmon fishing, it's different people with different views, and it really depends with whom you learn. It just goes to show how much of a mystique there is about the sport. Here are two highly respected fishers with two very different opinions on a crucial subject and each with their own followers.

So let's assume you have struck, and the fish is well and truly hooked! The next step is to play him, a rather unfortunate term, I always think, as this is not a game. What it means is that your fish will obviously be trying to get off the hook while you are attempting to get him to the shore. You'll find that, just as salmon take in different ways, they also react differently to being caught. I've noticed that some stronger, fresher fish go completely crazy, careering up and down a pool and diving in and out of the water, whereas others may come quietly and allow themselves simply to be led to the bank. Again, the various experts will tell you different ways to play a fish, but I shall try to pass on the advice that was given to me as a beginner.

Firstly, keep in contact with your fish. This is done by keeping the rod-tip up, the line taut and the hook well embedded. It makes sense, if you think about it, for, if the line was slack, you'd have no real feel as to where he was going and you might also be giving him the chance to work the hook loose. I was also told that if a fish wants to run, then I should let him by spooling out some line and allowing him to go. The object of the battle is to tire him out, unless he tires you out first, which is always a possibility. There are fishers who have played a salmon for several hours before aching arms and throbbing backs force them to concede defeat. Then they must simply cut the nylon and their losses. But what a horrible though; not just the idea of losing the fish, but the fact that it must swim off with a hook embedded in its mouth!

'Keep your rod-tip up! Don't let him get upstream of you! Wind in, wind out!'. When you hook your first salmon, or any thereafter, there will hopefully be no shortage of folk around to give advice. The instructions will be endless, but at some stage, whether it's a few minutes or a few hours, you'll wind in and suddenly, you'll feel less resistance. It appears that you've tired your salmon out and he may even be coming slowly towards you.

Now you are about to land him, but don't be surprised if on approaching the bank, he suddenly senses danger and takes off again. These fish have great stamina and resilience and the fight is by no means over yet! I once watched a fellow angler reel in a fish that looked for all the world like it was spent, but each time it came in sight of the gravel bank, it gave an impassioned lurch, kicked its tail and was off again. He played it for over an hour and did eventually bring it to the bank, but he must have despaired of ever doing so!

There are ways of making things easier, though. There was a fisher on the Oykel in Sutherland who'd hooked a fair-sized salmon but was in all sorts of trouble as it threatened to take off out of the immediate pool and run downriver. 'Don't fight him, walk him up gently', said our host at the time. It was amazing to watch. Keeping an even pres-

How it should be done. My father-in-law being assisted by Jim, the ghillie on the Cassley

sure on the fish, but without touching the reel, our frazzled angler was shown how to walk slowly up the bank, while the salmon followed meekly in his wake, back into the centre of the pool. Of course, once the fish was within sight, he was far easier to control and eventually bring in.

Indeed, when you have a salmon on the end of your line, you'll have all sorts of worries to deal with. For example, will the nylon hold? Did you tie on your fly properly, or will that too work loose? Will the rod, which is straining like mad break in half? Will the fish pull so hard that he'll simply straighten the hooks and work himself free? The list of things that can go wrong is endless, however, on this occasion, let us be optimistic and assume that everything is tied correctly and does hold and that your rod, despite being bent double, doesn't snap. In fact, you really seem to be getting the upper hand and your fish is tiring.

Now, for the next crucial bit and, again, let's assume that as a beginner you will have help. You've played out the fish and you've brought him to the bank and now you'll need your net. If it's lying further up the bank ask your helper to retrieve get it — remember to be courteous even in the excitement and do try not to move from your spot or you may spoil things! When he returns, ask him or her to slide the net under the water while you bring the fish to the surface and lead it gently across the current and into the net. Now your helper must lift net and fish out of the water and onto the bank. This sounds a simple operation, but it can easily go wrong. Landing a fish can be a minefield, and even the experts have their off-days.

One spring night on the River Tay, whilst most of the party had retired to the hut for a dram, my husband was bravely soldiering on by the water's edge. Suddenly, a salmon! He was fishing from a steep bank and there was no way he could bring in this thing on his own, so he started shouting and yelling for help. But the party in the hut was in full swing and it was a good 20 minutes and several drams later before the ghillie popped his head round the hut door.

'Rod, you've got a fish on!' he exclaimed. 'Don't worry now, I'll be right with you.' And with that, he went back into the hut. Eventually, after what seemed like an eternity, he reappeared with a large salmon net and started tottering rather uncertainly down to the riverside. It should all have been so easy. The fish was lying spent in the pool below the bank and all the ghillie had to do was to take the net and carefully whisk him out. But, by this stage, his normally impeccable Scottish aim wasn't quite so keen and, as he fumbled about in the water, he somehow managed to knock the hook out of the salmon's mouth with the side of the net. My husband recalls it as if it were a slow motion flashback and he still remembers the awful moment when he and the ghillie could only stand and watch as the fish, sensing freedom, flicked his tail, waved good-bye and disappeared into the darkness. Rod felt terrible, but you can imagine that the poor ghillie felt far worse. The only course of action was to return to the hut and take a few more drams. This is when the medicinal qualities of Scotch are most needed.

Wrong again!

It can happen to anyone. A girlfriend of mine had hooked a salmon and called for help, so in I went, full of enthusiasm and raring to go. Never having done it before, but recalling butterfly-hunting days in

Africa, I was fully confident as I went about it in a similar way, that is, trying to net the fish from above! Needless to say, my friend's shrieks of horror stopped me in mid-air before any serious damage was done! In fact, I don't think I'm a very good netter, full stop. There was the time when Rod and I arrived to fish the Dee in late spring. We were told there were lots of fish around, so after a quick pub supper, we hurried down to the water to catch the last of the evening light. Five minutes into the proceedings, there was a splash and a triumphant call as Rod shouted for the net. I'd got it the right way up this time, you'll be relieved to hear, but I'm short-sighted and by now it was nearly dark, so I couldn't for the life of me see what I was doing or where I was going. 'Get out of the water!' my husband shouted as I stumbled myopically about in the pool. 'You're standing on the line! Get out of the water, Fiona!' Here it's worth repeating that partnerships really can be made or broken when fishing. In our case, I would just say that the glue's been tested a few times! Anyway, to everyone's relief, the story had a happy ending, as Rod netted his own fish and then did the same for me when I caught a spanking nine pounder half-an-hour later.

And he was right, for if there's the slightest doubt that the person who's helping might make a mess of things, you must do the job yourself. So, hold your rod in your right hand, (unless you're left-handed of course) and the net firmly in the other. (Here might be good time to mention that some folk suggest keeping a stone in the bottom of the net to weigh it down, which seems a good idea, as, theoretically, it should keep the net steady and stop it turning inside-out). Now put the net in the water and slowly bring the fish over the top of it. It's a good idea to make sure that there are no large rocks in the water which might get in your way but again, the main thing is to get your catch out onto the bank as quickly as possible.

When you land your first salmon, there will always be a degree of panic, but hopefully you'll either have a competent helper or a net with you. When you catch your second there will still be some panic, but Murphy's Law will decree that your helper has just gone home and your net is in the car a quarter-of-a-mile away. So, beginner or not, you must now learn to land a fish without either. It sounds difficult, but I promise you, it's not as hopeless as it seems.

Quite simply, if you find yourself in this predicament, try to look for somewhere to beach the fish, either on a spit of gravel or perhaps a grassy ledge by the water's edge. Again, make sure the fish is played out. What you have to do is to find your chosen spot, wind in some line, walk him to the landing spot and gently pull your fish out of the water onto the grass or gravel. He'll probably struggle a little as he touches

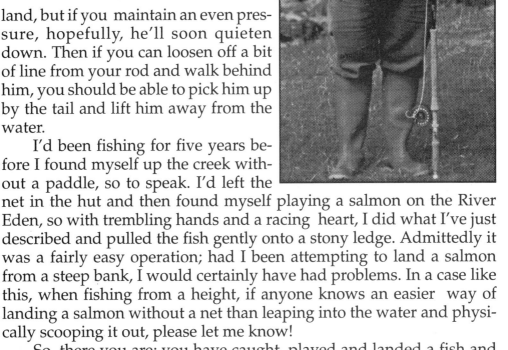

Christopher Fryer with a newly-landed salmon...and right, dad Andrew proving that even the grown-ups can do it!

land, but if you maintain an even pressure, hopefully, he'll soon quieten down. Then if you can loosen off a bit of line from your rod and walk behind him, you should be able to pick him up by the tail and lift him away from the water.

I'd been fishing for five years before I found myself up the creek without a paddle, so to speak. I'd left the net in the hut and then found myself playing a salmon on the River Eden, so with trembling hands and a racing heart, I did what I've just described and pulled the fish gently onto a stony ledge. Admittedly it was a fairly easy operation; had I been attempting to land a salmon from a steep bank, I would certainly have had problems. In a case like this, when fishing from a height, if anyone knows an easier way of landing a salmon without a net than leaping into the water and physically scooping it out, please let me know!

So, there you are; you have caught, played and landed a fish and now that he's on the bank, a decision must be made. Game fishers have traditionally killed and eaten their catches, but these days there's a small but growing trend to put fish back. I have to say that I don't agree with this policy, I'm afraid. I would return a very small fish, I would return a kelt or a salmon that looked very red or black, or which looked like it was just about to spawn. I would also return a fish that had been foul-hooked, that is, hooked somewhere other than in the mouth since both fishing law and etiquette demand that you must return such a fish. Any other salmon, however, I would, and do, keep.

I don't know what I'd have done though, if I'd been in our friends' place on the River Tay last year. Whilst fishing happily from a boat, a huge salmon suddenly leapt from the water and landed right in the boat. They sportingly put it back, but I ask myself, would I have done the same if I'd been fishing all day and caught nothing? The chances are that I shall never be faced with such a quandary, thank God!

It's just that I don't want to play with a fish simply for the fun and excitement of the struggle. No, to my mind, a healthy fish that's caught fairly should be eaten. Whichever way you decide though, it must be done quickly and if you choose to keep him, he must be despatched as humanely as possible. The worst thing you can end up doing is to stand about dithering while you make up your mind.

The proper instrument used to kill a fish is a priest, so named be-cause in medieval times, priests in battle were not allowed to draw blood, so used clubs instead of swords! It resembles a small heavy truncheon, but if you don't have one to hand, then a heavy stone or a sturdy piece of wood can often do the job just as well. Take whatever you're using, roll the fish over onto his stomach and give a couple of short, sharp taps to the head just above the eyes. That should suffice. Now cover him up, or put him in a bag, away from sun or flies.

Your first salmon! When you get to this stage, you'll either be filled with remorse and vow never to kill a living thing again, or you'll feel great elation, a sense of achievement and long to get back to the water to catch another. If you fail to land a fish, terms which might help cheer you up are a 'pull' or a 'touch' and these are very heartening for a salmon fisher, because if either of these occur it means that a fish has toyed with the fly and maybe sucked it in and then let it go. Whichever way, at least there's been some interest, so your fly must have looked lifelike and appetizing. If you get some reaction from the water, you may have 'moved' or 'raised' a fish, all common terms you'll hear in angling, for it's certainly better to have had a bite than nothing at all! I was out on the Border Esk one evening when nothing was being taken and no-one saw anything but at least I got a pull and very exciting it was too as the rod juddered and shook and the fish gave a little leap before disap-pearing into the darkness. That was all I had that night, but it was more than most had.

One final thought to help you in your quest. We've talked about good places and good times to fish, but are there really such things as perfect fishing conditions? Well, I've asked various friends and here are a few thoughts. Everyone, it seems has different ideas on when and where you're most likely to be successful.

'Fish after a spate when the river is dropping, because salmon are roused into activity and are being drawn upstream.'

'Salmon don't like the glare of the sun, so they tend to sit in shady places.'

'Salmon are most likely to take a fly when they're resting in a pool, not running.'

'They move in the dark, so night time or early morning can be good taking times.'

'Rain is good, and a most magical taking time is when a river first begins to rise, after a heavy downpour or melting snow.'

Everyone seems to agree that, for success, the air should be warmer than the water. Also, very important for a beginner, or for any angler, is the advice not to put yourself out when conditions are really bad, because you'll just end up getting frustrated and annoyed and that's the worst thing, because fishing shouldn't be a bore!

Looking after your equipment

I wonder if the fish goes home and boasts about the size of the bait he stole.

Anon

*I*f you've got this far, you'll have realised by now that salmon fishing isn't cheap, so it's really worth looking after your equipment. The nice thing about angling is that there are several million of us, so we shouldn't ever be short of a companion or two, even as a fly-fisher. We are often to be found in groups in cars and huts, with our bags and clothes all heaped together too. So, as a beginner, with lots of lovely new tackle, it's worth marking things to make them more identifiable.

Writing a name on the inside of each boot is a good idea and I wish I had when I first started fishing, as somewhere along the way, I've ended up with different-sized thigh waders. I'm a size seven, but at some stage we've obviously fished with someone who was a size eight, so now I'm the proud owner of one of each. That's not too bad: at least I can fill out the larger size by wearing an extra pair of socks. It's the person who's now having to squeeze his or her size eight into my size seven who must really be suffering!

Also mislaid last year was a jacket; a much loved, tatty, green one, lost in Cumbria by the river Eden. Put down on a grassy verge, never to be seen again. Actually it wasn't so much the jacket but the contact lenses in the pocket which I really missed. However, that's a lesson. Had I been wearing them I might not only have been able to see where I'd left the jacket, I might also have spotted a few more fish! Still, that's not as bad as some people we know who left hundreds of pounds worth of new tackle in an unlocked car in a nearby lane while they surveyed their chosen river and when they returned, it wasn't just the car radio that was missing. It's a wretched thing to think that you have to be on your guard even in the countryside, but times are changing and it's wise to be security-conscious.

You see, folk get very attached to their angling bits and bobs, though some get more attached than others and with good reason too. My dear friend, Commander William Donald, a former naval officer and an ardent fisher who now lives in Cumbria, had something probably very few folk could ever boast about; not that he ever did because, Willie is very much a gentleman who just simply doesn't make a song and dance about such things. Now, had it been me, I would have been crowing about it to anyone who'd listen! There we were, talking about prized fishing possessions as we sat by the Border Esk one day, when he told me casually and quietly, that his most precious item had been a blue-green, high-necked jumper. Nothing remarkable in that, apart from the fact that its knitter was someone a bit special! It's a lovely tale. It was the start of the Second World War and every good woman in the land who wasn't busy digging was frantically knitting, carefully unravelling battered and holed jumpers and scarves to make new ones for the regulars and volunteers in the army, navy and air force. At that time,

Willie was up in Scotland, preparing to set sail on board his ship, when a crate arrived, filled with these small, but hugely welcome tokens. They were gratefully received by all the servicemen, but especially by the seamen, for a winter on the ocean could get to even the hardest soul. Well, the knitwear was duly distributed; amongst the items a scarf from an old lady in Southampton and a cardigan from three sisters in Manchester. But when Willie came to don his knitted offering, a beautiful thick jumper, he happened to see a small note pinned to the inside. It read: 'With best wishes from Her Majesty the Queen, Buckingham Palace, 1939'. He wore it proudly and that jumper kept Willie warm and safe throughout the war, even surviving the torpedoing of his ship.

When the fighting finished and there was time to turn to lighter things, the royal jumper went where the Queen Mother, a keen fisher herself, would probably most liked to have seen it go. It became Willie's fishing jumper, a prized and warm woollen and once again, a lucky one. He was wearing it when he caught his first salmon, appropriately fishing on royal Deeside, and he wore it to catch many, many more.

Sadly, the famed jumper is no more. Had it been around, it could have been snapped up by a museum, for I don't know how many jumpers the Queen Mother has knitted in her time, but it can't be a great number, surely? No, when it became too holed and snagged to stand any more wet and windy fishing days, a decision had to be made. What on earth was to be done with the Queen Mother's jumper? Well, they couldn't possibly throw it in the dustbin, so after much thought, Willie decided it should have a respectful end and the bits of wool that did remain were solemnly and carefully cremated in his garden.

Willie guarded that jumper jealously for many long fishing years and was especially careful not to leave it anywhere or lend it to anyone. You see, the problem is that after a bit of wear and tear, things like angling jumpers and hats tend to end up looking the same. Having said that, this sort of clothing is generally hardy and should stand some punishing treatment, but we can still do our bit to prolong its life.

For example, waders and wellies need to be properly dried out after each outing, and that means hanging them up. I've learned the hard way that if they're left on the floor in a crumpled heap, they either start to rot or they dry all creased, which means the fabric is much more likely to crack and inevitably leak. When putting waders away for the day, hang them on a hook. Upside down is the best way, and some pairs come with special hangers, or boot clips which attach to the sole. Failing that, you could use some good old-fashioned string. A warm place like a boiler room is an excellent place to dry out wet waders, but don't do what a friend of ours did, and leave them by the fire. Rubber melts, and quite quickly too!

Keeping boots off floor level stops unwelcome visitors. We know someone who left his waders in a garage cupboard for the winter, only to come back at the start of the fishing season to find a family of field mice nesting in the feet. Rather a sweet tale, I suppose, if only they hadn't chewed up the expensive, felt-lined soles to make a nice, cosy bed! Such a thing is unlikely to happen in our house since our black cat Max makes it his life's work to kill any living thing which happens to be smaller than he is. The moral here is shake out your boots before you put them on, even in the Scottish Borders. As children in Africa we learned to do this early on, so I'm an old hand at it, for if you left shoes out at night a scorpion might decide to rest there, ready to bite the foot that invaded its territory in the morning.

When you think of it, though, there's also another very good reason to hang up waders, and that's a social one! Fishing can be hot, sweaty work, and I defy anyone encased in rubber to plod for miles, then fish for hours and still come up smelling of roses. The funny thing is, you can get so carried away with the day that you often don't realise what's happening. A couple of years ago, I was completely baffled on the final day of a most enjoyable fishing trip on the Scottish west coast. There had been something in the air for the last few hours and I just couldn't put a name to it. Was it damp earth...? The water not as fresh as it should have been...? The hotel dog...? Anything and everything was getting blamed and it was only when the smell followed me into the hotel bar at the end of the day, that I realised what had happened! Needless to say, the offending articles, (socks, waders, etc...) were completely dried out and thoroughly aired, though it has to be said that some boots never recover and I'm afraid those took on a permanent smell, which I lived with for a few weeks until family and friends complained so bitterly that I felt I really had to buy a new pair.

A final note on waders: don't expect them to last forever because however careful you are, they are prone to wear and tear. Their life can be extended, though, with a wader mending kit, which is a useful little box of tricks consisting of patches of plastic or rubber which are glued over the offending rip. Alternatively, I've just discovered some liquid mender which comes out of a tube like toothpaste and then hardens over the hole. And pretty good stuff it is too, as I've used some on my watering can which was leaking at the seams and is now as good as new.

And so to jackets, which are rather more resilient than waders, but they too deserve a bit of kindness. If you fish, there's a very good chance that you'll get wet and it's surprising how long a sodden waxed jacket takes to dry out completely. There is, after all, nothing worse than going back a few days later to find a mouldy, damp offering and a waxed jacket will need to be re-waxed at some stage if it's to stay waterproof. Some of the more expensive makes can be sent back to the manufacturers to be done professionally, but if you follow the manufacturer's instructions you can have a go yourself. Be warned, however, it's not a job for the fainthearted!

So here it is, the Armstrong method for re-waxing a jacket. Take one can of special wax, (which can be bought from a tackle shop for a couple of pounds or so), find a warm place, and be prepared to use plenty of elbow grease. First, gently heat the jacket; either over a radiator, in a warming oven such as an Aga, or next to a boiler. Then, when it's nicely toasted, you need to rub in the wax with a stiff cloth over a newspaper (this is quite a messy affair). Next, simply pop it on a coathanger and leave it in a warm place for several hours, to give the wax time to sink into the fabric. Do keep it away from other clothes at this point since you certainly don't want to end up with wax on your best suit! And that's about it; you'll find it really gives a jacket a facelift. Obviously not the same professional look as sending it to the manufacturers, but there's definitely a feeling of satisfaction when you see this faded, crinkled old thing that you've bashed about in all year suddenly take on some of its original, deep colour.

As for other fishing clothes, look after your bits and pieces and they'll last much longer. If gloves, socks, hats, etc get wet, put them in the drier, by the fire, or in the airing cupboard. When the next time comes to fish you'll be glad that you did. In the same vein, don't leave soaked accessories in pockets or bags, as things like hankies go off pretty quickly.

Watch for tears and rips too as woolly socks and jumpers are easily pulled when fishing. Just climb a few barbed wire fences or get too near a large treble hook and you'll know what I mean. And if things do rip, it's worth sewing them sooner rather than later, before they get out of hand. I left something for a few months and a tiny hole became a great one, which meant my favourite fishing jumper was consigned to the cat basket. Even the cat turned its nose up as its smell promised something that it never delivered!

Remember to protect your equipment by making it easy to identify. For example, a rod can be marked with an indelible pen. These days, however, if it's stolen the chances of getting it back are slim as my friend with the unlocked car found out. Don't forget that tackle can be insured and it's probably well worth doing. What I've always been told is simply not to tempt fate, or thieves, by leaving expensive equipment obviously on display in the back of an unlocked car, or unattended by the river.

Recognising your own rod is one thing, as rods are pretty personal things, but as I mentioned earlier, put reels and flies together and they can all look much of a muchness, easily ending up in someone else's tackle box. Bigger items such as a reel should be fairly easy to mark in some way, but you obviously can't do this with 40 or so flies and 50 metres of nylon. And to be quite honest, it would look a bit Scrooge-like to arrive at the river having tagged every hook, line and sinker. So, as far as these smaller items are concerned, just be careful when it comes to collecting everything together at the end of the day. Bags, baskets and fly boxes all look fairly similar, and you don't want to give stuff away, do you?

In the same way, do try to return lent tackle, no matter how small and inexpensive it might seem, because people do remember and they might not be quite so eager to help out next time. I've lost count of the number of borrowed lures I've lost, but I would hope I always pay my dues, either with new stuff or compensatory drams.

Borrowing flies and hooks are one thing, but borrowing a rod is quite another; rods are not only prized, but pricey. Anyone who's lucky enough to have a modern, carbon-fibre rod will appreciate it being ul-tra-light and easy to carry, but it's also easily broken and the slightest knock can leave it, and you, shattered. Therefore, when travelling to the river, make sure it's in a safe place, somewhere where it can't be sat on or squeezed. I know it's very tempting in all the excitement and hurry just to throw it into the back of the car, but it's worth remember-ing that even if a rod's not actually broken, even a small bump can cause it to crack and weaken and the next time a line is cast, you may end up bitterly disappointed.

Again, when the rod's up, watch where it's put. That is, not on the ground where someone might accidentally stand on it and snap it, or in a place where it might slide over and break. I remember a morning on a small spate river when a party of fishers were discussing the height of the water and the state of the day when someone let out a cry of horror and all heads spun round to see a beautiful and expensive 15 footer slowly slide off the bonnet of a nearby car. Despite a desperate rush and grab by its owner, this £300 classic ended up on the ground, completely shattered.

So do watch where you put your rod and remember that when the rod's taken down, the proper place for it is in a sleeve. The solid metal or leather tubes will protect it from most things, but a basic cloth cover is certainly much better than nothing and should save any scratching or chipping. Again if you're in a hurry, I know it's tempting to throw the rod in the back of the car and think, 'Oh, I'll put it away later.' Al-ways put it away at once, making sure that the butt end stands down-wards and the tip end points upwards. This way the fragile tip is less likely to get damaged. I know I'm sounding very virtuous here and to be honest, every fisher has dropped or knocked over a rod at some stage, with varying results and, touch wood, mine doesn't seem to have suf-fered any permanent damage for the odd mishap, but then you never know. The next fishing trip could be the one that leaves me cursing and that is not a good thing. According to a 17th century proverb, 'If you swear you will catch no fish'. Now that explains why I've had so many blank days!

One final thought on your rod. It's a good idea when you're carrying it to hold it by the butt, with the rod-tip pointing backwards. It means you're less likely to poke somebody's eye out and you're also less likely to break the fragile tip end by bumping into a tree. I've also found that carrying it this way reduces the risk of getting the line tangled up in overhanging branches.

And so to reels which are hardier than rods, but again, neglect them at your peril! I once arrived at the river, eager to fish, only to find the spool grinding away in a most disconcerting way, so I thought I'd better investigate and when I opened it out, the inside was all rusted up. Well, of course, my first reaction was, 'Now, who did this?!', but then, thinking back, I recalled my previous fishing trip when I'd slipped off a rock into the river and given both rod and reel a thorough soaking. And then when I got home, I thought, 'Oh, I'll leave it, it'll dry out on its own.' It obviously hadn't and it was a painful lesson; the fishing conditions had been excellent, the weather was just right, the water teemed with fish but I only had the one reel with me, so the day was wasted! The moral is, keep your tackle dry when it's not in use and remember that a drop of oil or grease keeps everything turning.

And if reels are wary of water, they simply hate sand, so never put tackle down anywhere grainy, because before you know where you are, it's just like grinding peppercorns! I remember working with a newspaper photographer who wanted to take a snap of me sitting on the sand in my waders, and being an obliging soul, I duly posed. It was only when he sent me a selection of the prints that I realised to my despair that my rod and reel were also sitting there in the sand, getting nicely gritted up. Thank goodness that picture wasn't used in the paper otherwise I'd have been criticised by every angler in the land!

Ideally, equipment should be checked after every fishing trip, but the end of the season is a time for the angler to take stock of what he's got, what's missing or what needs repairing. When those boots are hung up as winter comes on, it's good to make sure that everything is left spick and span for your return in the spring.

Therefore, as soon as the season's over, make a checklist. Do it straightaway, otherwise you'll probably forget, especially in the run-up to Christmas. It might involve examining flies and ordering new ones to make sure they come in time for the New Year; or checking hooks, to see that all barbs are present and correct and not bent. It's very tempting to keep stuff that's nearly perfect and I am an old hoarder, I admit it, but sometimes it just doesn't pay. For example, if a fly started off with three hooks and now only has two, then I would throw it out. If I didn't, I know what would happen: I'd be fishing away happily and hook this real spring beauty, playing it for half an hour or so, my heart in my mouth, and then as I started to wind in — bang! The line would go loose and the fish would be away. Then there would be the agonizing. 'Oh, how could I have lost it?!', when really, it stands to reason that when a fly has a broken hook, all the fish has to do is to is shake its head and spit it out.

In the same way, it pays to make sure that hook barbs aren't blunt. I use the side of a matchbox to keep them nice and sharp, but a piece of emery cloth or board is probably the proper way to do it. Check fly-feathers too. I have one, my lucky fly, which is a yellow and brown creation that's served me well over the last couple of years, but unfortunately it's now nearly bald. I still use it from time to time, mainly out of hope and sentimentality, but a damaged fly is no longer the fly you once fished with.

Of course, it's possible to mend flies, and also to make them, but you have to have lots of patience and a steady hand and also a fair bit of spare time. Still, if you're lucky enough to have all three, it's worth having a go at fly-tying and keen fishers tell me they spend many a happy hour doing just that. Our friend, Mike Clough, another ace salmon fisher, made me a beautiful pattern in blue and black which we Christened the Fifi fly. It's not caught anything yet, although with a name like that, it should attract something, surely? Then there's young Jamie Hammond, who, not content with catching huge fish, is now turning his fly-tying into a cottage industry, churning them out and flogging them to friends and family. They work too. Rod's father ordered a box-full and one of them immediately hooked a fish! It was on the River Dee, the Bellwade pool, so Jamie's fly became the 'Bellwade Special'.

As for the heavier tackle, at the end of the year it's wise to check rods and rod-rings for signs of cracking. If they're all right, they can be wiped down and carefully placed back in their sleeves. Reels should be dismantled and lightly oiled. Line should be checked for kinks and frays, but, let's face it, you'd have to be a pretty heavy-handed fisher to get through a whole line in one season.

As far as leader goes, most experts recommend that any nylon that's left at the end of the year should be thrown away, for it can easily rot and weaken. If you want to be safe rather than sorry, the advice is to buy a new lot at the start of each fishing season. If you must keep the old stuff for a second year, be it on your own head and keep it away from heat and sunlight to give it a sporting chance of surviving another season.

And if you want to survive another season, it's probably a good idea to clear out debris from tackle bags and boxes at the end of the year; since you'll be surprised at what accumulates over the fishing months. Corners of corned-beef sandwiches, sticky toffee papers, ragged bits of old tissue, broken hooks, a dried-up apple or even a flask of three-month old coffee are some of the things I've discovered. I remember in particular at the start of one fishing year my husband came into the kitchen, clutching my fishing bag and what looked suspiciously like a bag of stinking rubbish. On closer examination, that's exactly what it was! All the above things I've mentioned plus a few more mouldy bits and pieces. At long last, we'd tracked down the reason for the awful smell in the understairs cupboard! Which just goes to show that like everything else in fishing, you must take responsibility for your own kit. Then if your waders leak, or your line snaps, or if you let your tackle bag get completely out of hand, you've only yourself to blame.

Safety on the water

One, two, three, four, five
Once I caught a fish alive.
Why did I let it go?
Because it bit my finger so.

Anon

*N*ow, while it's most unlikely that you'll get bitten, you might well get your fingers burnt, for there are dangers in fishing. 'Dangers, what dangers? Unlike some sports — motor racing, rugby, etc. — fishing's a relaxing, safe way to pass the time, isn't it? Relaxing? More often than not. Safe? Well, I don't want to put you off, but not always. Fishing may be Britain's most popular participant sport, but it can certainly be dangerous, or at the least painful, so beware!

The first thing to remember is that in fishing, we're dealing with water and obvious as it sounds, it must be stressed that people can drown in water. Rivers are often deep and currents treacherous and great care is needed. It really came home to me a couple of years ago when Rod and I arrived to fish the River Tay near Perth to find our normally chatty ghillie full of doom and gloom, issuing dire warnings to anyone who went within a few yards of the waters edge. It turned out that he'd been looking after a party of happy-go-lucky fly-fishers, a group who came regularly each year in search of fresh spring salmon. They weren't novices by any stretch of the imagination, so he'd set up rods and placed them at various points along the beat. One of the party, a young man in his thirties, was never seen alive again. When the ghillie came back to check on him, he'd simply disappeared. His rod and hat were found floating close-by in the water, but it was several days before his body was recovered near the mouth of the river.

No-one will ever know exactly what happened. The Tay is a notoriously dangerous water, with deep pools and strong, swirling currents. One minute, you can be fishing in just a few inches of water, and the next step can take you well out of your depth. It obviously helps to be able to swim. But the best swimmer in the world is no match for a raging torrent and really, who would survive long in freezing water early in springtime? The point is, accidents and tragedies can and do happen. Even a stretch that you know to be harmless can turn nasty, and familiarity breeds contempt, as they say.

Again, fishing from a boat may seem peaceful enough, but again, there are the horror stories. My husband and his father were once inspecting business sites in Perthshire when they came upon a remote hill loch. As they walked over the crest of the hill they noticed a couple of Land Rovers and a police van complete with diving team. It appeared that this angler had hooked a fish whilst sitting in the boat and in the excitement to play it, he'd stood up, overbalanced and fallen in. The divers were there to collect his body.

Those are drastic and horrible examples, I know, but I'm sure that almost every fisher can tell of his own personal scare in the water, usually not helped by wearing great cumbersome waders. They're awkward things at the best of times, but just imagine trying to swim in them!

The moral is, therefore, caution at all times and unless you know the river, it probably makes sense to wear a life-jacket. This is a lightweight life-saver and comes with a variety of pockets, so it'll be useful, reassuring, and will also provide an extra layer in winter. I have to admit to spending my first fishing years without one, since I was brought up a strong swimmer and couldn't see the need most of the time. But despite that, after the sobering tale from the Tay, my husband went out to the nearest tackle shop and bought us each a life-jacket and now if conditions look dodgy, I wouldn't be without it.

A life jacket might have proved quite useful for the elderly woman who got into trouble up in Aberdeenshire a couple of years ago. It was lunchtime and after an exhilarating but fishless morning, this grand old lady climbed into her car, ready to take her three dogs, all happily sitting on the back seat, home for a feed. So she started the engine and found first gear, then disaster! Unfortunately, she was still wearing her waders and one of the boots got jammed between the accelerator and the side of the footwell, sending the car hurtling into the river. All hell let loose and I really don't know who got the biggest shock, the old lady, the dogs or a nearby ghillie who was minding his own business eating his lunch on the bank. He just couldn't believe his eyes, but quick as a flash, he jumped into the water, grabbed the car bumper and tried to steer the still-floating car back towards the shore. The poor ghillie. He was in a real state, not least because he was up to his neck in freezing water, but he feared the worst for the car's occupants. He shouldn't have worried — old ladies, especially old lady fishers, are made of sterner stuff and there she was, sitting calmly in her seat calling out instructions as the car floated slowly downstream.!

The trick is to avoid falling in at all, with or without a car. Wading on slimy and slippery stones can be a minefield, but there are aids to help the angler stay upright and so preserve dignity at least! First-off are boots with felt anti-slip soles; expensive for sure, but then how much do you value your life? Another life saver is the wading stick which looks like a long pole, often made of wood or plastic, and is used to feel the way along a river bottom or as a "steady" when the current gets rough. There are many different sticks on the market, but a good one should be sturdy and weighted at the bottom end so it doesn't float away in the stream. If that happens, you'll spend half your time trying

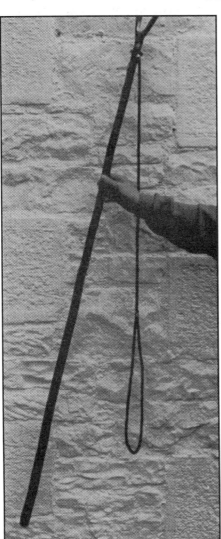

to retrieve the stick, rather than actually fishing. A good stick will also have a loop at the top, which slips over the shoulder when it's being carried. Some people make their own, out of a branch or a length of wood, but do make sure that it's weighted and robust. It's no good if the thing's going to snap in mid-stream.

Again, I'm ashamed to say that I've only recently bought myself a wading stick and that's after a few frights on slippery stones. Somehow, when you start fishing for salmon, you're keen to buy the exciting things, like the rod and the reel, but the life-jackets and wading sticks just don't seem that glamorous or necessary. Any experienced fisher will tell you that they're not just necessary, they're a vital part of the kit. So don't make the mistake of thinking that fishing aids are just for the doddery and old. Water is no respecter of age, any age.

Take a leaf out of an old sailor's book. I know a former sea-captain who regularly fishes, but always with a life jacket and wading stick. The advice that

My wading-stick. An essential accessory

was given to me, which I pass on to you, is never to underestimate the power of the river or get too familiar or daring. I've been caught out on several occasions, when I've waded into a stretch of water I thought I knew well, only to find myself suddenly in a fierce stream which nearly knocked me off my feet. Without a stick, I've tried to turn back and been paralysed by the force of the current. It's a scary feeling, even for a school backstroke champion!

One final thought; if you do find yourself up the creek without a paddle, or upstream without a stick, and if you're carrying your net, you can always improvise with that by holding the round end and using the handle as a steady until you reach the shallows. Meanwhile if you find yourself stickless and netless and really in a jam, you can always use your rod to steady you home and this I've done, although it doesn't do much for the reel and should be considered a last resort. If you break the rod and get to the bank, you can always buy a new one. If you break it and don't make it, it won't matter anyway. However, we're assuming that you do make it, so remember to wipe down your rod, dry your reel and grease it!

Touch wood (or carbon-fibre), I've only once fallen in properly. Fishing the River Eden in Cumbria a couple of years ago, I waded out into the shallows and slipped on a slimy rock. Luckily it wasn't deep or dangerous, but I still ended up crouched on all fours in the water. The worst bit was the indignity of it all, trying to steady myself without breaking the rod or losing the net! Anyway, I managed to hold onto the tackle and the rod survived intact, but I was soaked through. Stupidly, I'd no change of clothing, and we were too far from home to return and get a spare set, so rather than waste the day and to the great amusement of our host and a couple of fishers on the opposite bank, I stripped off to my underwear and dried out everything on the car roof-rack! Such things happen when you're fishing, but really, you don't want to put yourself in the position where you might end up with pneumonia or an unwelcome audience. My fishing experience has taught me that anglers need caution and commonsense and that means judging the pools and, if they're too deep for comfort, not risking it. Don't forget also that water levels rise and what's safe at midday might not be so at teatime.

We heard a salutary tale from the Achness Hotel in Sutherland, about a party of fishers who'd had an unfortunate experience eight miles upstream on the River Cassley. They'd taken a boat across the water, and when they set off, levels were low, but it was a pouring-wet day with gale-force winds and before they knew it the river started rising. They couldn't get back to the boat and ending up marooned on the far bank. Later that afternoon, when they didn't report back to the hotel, an alert went out and eventually a helicopter was brought in to rescue them. However because of the wind it couldn't land and so the hapless anglers spent a miserable night huddled together until 16 hours later they were brought to safety by the inshore lifeboat crew. Quite a way to end what should have been an enjoyable day on the river.

Something like that makes you think of safety in general and as I write this book as a new mother, my thoughts turn to something I've never given much time to in the past, children. I'm not sure that children and fishing go well together until they're old enough to wield a rod, but as we're discovering, family lunches by the river can be wonderful fun. Any parent will tell you that water holds a great fascination for children and the fact remains that a child can drown in just an inch or so. The problem is that fishing is a totally absorbing sport, and once you get going, there's a tendency to think of very little else, so this year if I take baby along to the river, I'll also have someone there who's not fishing and who can keep a watchful eye.

These are some of the dangers of wate. Now let's look at the equipment, because fishing tackle can do a fair bit of damage. Take a fly-hook, for example, Once a barb goes in it's nigh-on impossible to pull out and I speak from experience here. My husband and I were on the River Derwent in West Cumbria. It was late summer and an excellent fishing day; a little overcast with a slight breeze on the water and literally dozens of silvery salmon dancing around our feet. We'd been busy for half-an-hour or so, when Rod decided to try his luck further downstream. 'You're bound to catch something', he said cheerfully, as he ambled off to the next pool. How right he was.

I'd only been fishing for a year or so and normally I'd have panicked at the thought of being left so totally to my own devices, but having just mastered the art of tying knots, I felt pretty confident. A few over-energetic casts, and I'd lost the fly. Never mind, I started to put on another one and was just pulling the knot tight, when I tugged a little too enthusiastically and pulled the hook right into my index finger. Now being stabbed by a fishing barb certainly isn't the most pleasant experience and I know I wasn't laughing at the time, but looking back, it was quite comical. The fly had embedded itself in my flesh and instead of simply cutting it loose from line and rod, I ran a quarter of a mile down the river bank shouting for my better half, with fly, nylon, line and 14 foot salmon rod all hanging from my finger! When I found him, my husband took one look and calmly cut the line to free me from yards of superfluous tackle. Next we tried to get the hook out with a penknife but it just seemed to be going in deeper, so reluctantly we abandoned the job, all those lovely fish and set off for the local cottage hospital. By this stage I was quite distressed, though we had to laugh at the thought that, had I been on my own, I'd probably have turned up for treatment still attached to a massive salmon rod!

I thought I'd be a great novelty in the hospital with a gaily coloured salmon fly poking out of my finger, but these places it seems, are well prepared for hunters, fishers and shooters and they didn't bat an eyelid. Instead the nurse numbed the finger, pushed the hook through the skin, snipped off the barb with a pair of garden secateurs, '...saved specially for people like you!' and pulled the hook back through. A simple operation, I know, but to a born coward, it was pretty traumatic. The worst thing about it all was that they gave me an anti-tetanus jab. The finger was better the next day, but I had difficulty sitting down for a week! Needless to say, after this performance, we didn't return to the river, but made instead for the nearest pub, for some shock treatment!

I joke about it now, but it certainly taught me a lesson in safety when it comes to tying knots. It also made me realise that things could have been a lot worse because hooks have been known to enter cheeks, ears, even eyes. When the wind is blowing and the flies are flying, watch out! This is certainly one of the most dangerous times, when the angler is casting and throwing around lengths of line and nylon with a sharpened barb at the end. Wearing glasses, safety-glasses or sunglasses does help to protect eyes, and hats and scarves go some way to shielding faces and ears, but if you're casting, you just have to try to be aware of what's happening behind so you don't end up hooking some innocent passer-by. In the same vein, if you are watching someone cast, always make sure you stand well back. If you must stand close, that is, if you're being taught what to do, then I was always advise to tuck in as closely as possible to the opposite side of the shoulder that the caster is using. I was also told in no uncertain terms, never to sneak up behind another fisher when they're casting, but always to give some warning.

Just as I try to take care when casting with the rod, I also try to watch out when I'm carrying it. Remember, it's got a thin, pointed tip end which can easily poke out an eye, so it should always be carried with the point facing backwards. In the same vein, you should keep well back if you're following someone who's carrying a rod. Don't forget, 15 feet or so goes an awfully long way! Take care too when putting it up or waving it around. Modern, carbon-fibre rods are great conductors of electricity, and power lines are often low in country areas, especially in courtyards outside houses or hotels.

Beware too those electric fences, which seem to be as popular as ever with farmers these days. A mad keen fishing pal recalls many years ago going night fishing on the River Eden. Returning absolutely soaked in the dark, they came to a fence and as he grabbed hold to jump over he realised rather quickly it was electrified. His acrobatics as he was catapulted headfirst into the air would have put Daley Thompson to shame! Now electric fences I can cope with but the one thing I really I hate is being out in a storm when I'm fishing, because I have visions of the lightening striking the rod and burning me to a frazzle. It sounds melodramatic, I know, but it's not as impossible as it sounds, so if you do find yourself in an electric storm, the advice is to seek shelter as soon as possible.

On a less dramatic note, fishing involves following the country code and that means taking home litter, shutting farm gates and not starting fires. It also means watching out for animals, especially where cattle and sheep might be standing near the river bank where you're casting. For the same reason it's probably not a good idea to take a dog along to the water, because unless it's kept on a lead you may have problems. Mac, my sister-in-law's labrador, is a lovely fellow, a real black beauty of a dog, who's normally very well behaved, but one afternoon my father-in-law and I made the fatal mistake of taking him fishing. He should really have stayed at home, but he looked so sad with those eyes and you know what it's like! We'd not been at the water more than five minutes when Mac decided there were many more interesting things happening further down stream and so off he set in hot pursuit of a flight of wild duck. Needless to say, the fishing went by the board and we spent the rest of the afternoon in pursuit of the dog.

But if dogs are one thing, birds and other feathered creatures are quite another. A great friend of ours, Andrew Fryer, tells a story of how as a boy he was up to some alternative fly- fishing. Whilst out with his father and friends, he was determined to outfish them all, so he popped a nice juicy worm on the end of his hook and kept lengthening his line. Then, as he cast backwards he became a bit too adventurous and the line happened to touch the ground, where the worm was immediately pounced on by a passing hen. The next thing Andrew knew, he was fishing with line and chicken, as the poor bird came sailing overhead! Needless to say, that was a one-off and Andrew went on to become one of the finest fishers I know.

Finally, on the subject of animals, one of the most important rules in angling is not to leave bits of nylon lying about. When you change a line, take the old one home or cut it into tiny pieces and bury it. And if you find another angler's cast hanging from a tree, do take it down. It's another chore, I know, but it must be done as the careless throwing away of a length of nylon can cause great suffering to birds and small animals which may become entangled in it.

Another great peril of fishing is the dreaded midge! You can just see the scene. It's a quiet summer's evening and you're standing by the river, totally at peace with the world, when there's an invasion and you suddenly realise you're being attacked by hordes of biting insects. Clegs, big horse flies which give a wicked bite, are some of the most horrible things on this earth, so slap on the anti-midge oil before venturing out. I've found that people think of all manner of interesting ways to avoid the midges, but our friend, Andrew Fryer, has the most unconventional one I've ever seen. On a hot summer's night he can be spotted fishing away, complete with gloves, scarf, a beekeeper's hat and veil, with his pipe going full-tilt underneath. How he survives is hard to imagine!

I suppose that living near a river I'm becoming slightly immune to the little monsters. The thing is, I've been bitten so many times that I'm probably resigned to it all. Having said that, I always try to wear a hat when the midges are about because they make straight for my scalp and forehead, and that usually results in a huge cover-up job for the poor old make-up girls when I return to work in London. I've lost track of the number of times I've sat in the make-up chair, and heard the sigh, 'You've been fishing again I see!'

Nettles are not pleasant, nor are bee or wasp stings, but these are all part and parcel of country life...says she who was stung on the foot last week whilst foolishly walking across a field of clover in a pair of sandals. In such cases, I realise that it would pay to keep a small first-aid kit in the tackle-box.

Two other useful points: tell someone where you're heading when you go fishing, especially if you're on your own, or if it's at night. Then, if there's an accident and you do something awful, like break an ankle, at least someone can raise the alarm when you're not back. It's easy to lose track of time when fishing, especially if like me, you never wear a watch. I'm afraid I'm not very good at timekeeping; in fact I was the one who, in my radio days, informed the good listeners of the Thames Valley that it was 8.30am instead of 7.30am. (Listeners to Eddie Mair Live on BBC Radio Scotland will be probably quite impressed with my accuracy!) Thousands of commuters must have choked on their corn-flakes as they heard the news that they were late for work, including my boss, who wasn't amused!

Lastly, although fishing and alcohol can go very nicely together at certain times, whisky and water can be a lethal combination. So, even though it's tempting to celebrate a catch with something suitable, I have to say reluctantly that it's best to save the drams for the end of the day. Tell yourself that it's something to look forward to and you'll fish with a goal in mind, and go a lot more steadily in the water and on the bank. It goes without saying that you should not even consider a dram if you have the responsibility of driving back at the end of the day. There will be plenty of time for drams in the bar or in the house later, so please don't risk it.

And finally, please, please don't be put off by this chapter of gloom and possible doom. Fishing is a joy which I highly recommend. But like any other sport, there are certain rules to abide by. The main one, of course, is just to use some common sense. And if you think that all the safety equipment outweighs the fun of the sport, cheer up! You could be preparing for American Football instead!

Watch where you're putting it!

The ghillie, the hut, the tales

Do you think this is the best fly to catch a fish?
(Fisher)

Now, if I knew that for certain, I wouldn't be ghillying.
(Highland ghillie)

*A*n eccentric, a one-off or simply an ace angler. However you describe a ghillie, he remains a unique character and someone who deserves a chapter of his own. This is the man, or woman — yes, there is rumoured to be at least one female ghillie about — who's traditionally associated with game fishing.

Basically, the ghillie is the helper, employed by whoever owns the fishing. His job involves looking after visiting anglers during the fishing season. The rest of the year, his time may be spent improving pools, repairing paths or painting huts and boats. Dedicated to the banks and rivers he cares for, when he fishes with you his brief is a mixed one and can include tackling up, advising on what type of fly to use, taking out wind knots, changing leaders and untangling line. Sometimes, he may be someone who's been on the river for 30 years or more and he'll know every stone and stream of the water for which he cares, so he'll be able to show you exactly where to wade and cast. Of course, if you're fishing from a boat, he'll usually offer to row. He should know exactly where the fish are lying and be on hand to net that silvery

Boat fishing on the Upper Dunkeld beat, River Tay with ghillie John Mackenzie and Corrie, his dog

salmon when it takes your fly! He's learned his trade by the water's edge and, to my mind, he's the greatest asset an angler can possibly have.

The dictionary definition of a ghillie is, 'a sportsman's attendant, in the Highlands' and although I've come across boatmen and watermen who look after anglers in England and Wales, I'm told that the ghillie as such remains a thoroughly Scottish invention, so let's look at these wonderful characters.

From young John in his twenties on Deeside, to the 70 year-old gentleman I fish with on the Border Esk, they come in all ages. Youth has enthusiasm and energy, and age has a wealth of patience and knowledge; both are experiences not to be missed. Ghillies come from all walks of life, from Jim, the former shepherd who works the River Cassley in Sutherland to Alec, the one-time paratrooper, now ghillie on the neighbouring River Oykel. What brings them together is the joy of watercraft and a love of the great outdoors.

So what makes a good ghillie? I asked my friend, Willie Donald, he of the royal jumper and someone with more than 40 years' experience of salmon fishing, for his views. This is what he came up with.

'A good ghillie can make a day's fishing, even if it's a blank one; a not so good ghillie can spoil it. In my experience, the former are in the majority and I count some of them as the grandest of my friends. A ghillie's job is just a job, but by no means an easy one. He must know every inch of the water on which he fishes and give of his best to a visiting rod. This is not always easy if conditions are poor, or the visitor is a novice, or show-off type. At the same time he must remember that the guest's day on the river may be his or her only outing of the year, greatly looked forward to and brought to an end with reluctance.'

In short, if you're offered the services of a ghillie, jump at the chance! And do make sure you make proper use of it. I've talked to ghillies who say there's nothing worse than a silent fisher who never asks about what sort of fly to use, or where and how to fish a pool. What a waste! Even if it's a disappointing, blank day, a ghillie can be a great companion with whom to while away the time; most of them are great characters and will keep you amused for hours if you let them.

They're generally nature's gentlemen and are not only highly knowledgeable about the water and the fish, but may also have a wealth of facts at their fingertips about local plants and wildlife. Mind you, they'll want to know that you're taking it all seriously and paying attention to the job in hand. Like the Highland chap who tests you by letting you fish flyless for several minutes before asking innocently if you've noticed anything wrong with the line. Or the one who thought he'd liven things up for a fishless and despairing guest. Sensing that his charge, an accountant, was flagging, he crept up silently behind him and turfed a large rock into the water. Now any angler will tell you that the merest hint of a splash is guaranteed instantly to revive the most despondent fisher and, of course, the man turned round in high expectation. 'Well now, did you hear that sir?!' said the ghillie. 'A big fish, no doubt about that! If you carry on, I'm sure you'll have him.' And so he left his guest redoubling his efforts, flogging away in high expectation and went off down river. Revenge was sweet though and sometimes, just sometimes, we fishers do have the last laugh. When the ghillie returned, the accountant was beaming all over his face. 'Guess what', he said. 'I fished that spot, just like you suggested, and I caught it! Come and have a look, it's in the back of the car.' Amazed, the ghillie watched, as the man opened the boot to display his catch...a large rock!

It must be said here that both ghillie and fisher were old mates and well used to such tricks. As a beginner I can reassure you that it's unlikely that you'll come in for such treatment, especially if you can get your helper to take you under his wing. When I first worked with a ghillie I was mortified, thinking he'd be horrified at my feeble attempts at casting. But it's worth remembering that however awful you are, he's usually seen worse, so the best thing to do is to throw yourself onto his mercy. 'I haven't got much fishing experience but I'm always keen to learn, so tell me when I do something wrong' always goes down well. Ask him for advice and then take it! If he recommends a brown and yellow fly, try it. If you're successful, well and good, but if nothing's happening, then in due course a casual, 'Shall we try this one? It's always been a favourite of mine.' might be in order. A good ghillie will often agree because a good ghillie wants nothing more than to see you go home with a fish.

Some are more enthusiastic than others, like the former army man who marched me miles up and down the river for hour after hour, instructing me on how to cast and where to wade. It was the first week of the season so I wasn't as fit as I should have been and it was also my first time with a ghillie, so I really didn't know what to expect. When I got back to the hotel, I burst into tears. 'I'm not going out tomorrow,' I raged at my long-suffering husband. 'I ache all over, I'm sick of casting and wading and I hate fishing!'. Fishing can sometimes be all or nothing, you understand, and if you haven't fished for a while, a day's strenuous casting can leave you feeling pretty sore. Well, someone must have had a quiet word about this poor excuse for an angler and the next day was much more gentle. In fact I recall that we were even allowed to stop for lunch. So remember, his keenness must really be matched by yours and that's up to the two of you to work out.

But part of a ghillie's charm will be this enthusiasm, for it's his job to bolster morale. On the first day of a fishing trip, expectations are high and the water is fished hard. But come day three, you've not even had a touch and in desperation you finally turn to your helper to ask, 'Well, what do you think?'... then it's his responsibility to raise spirits. Normally the answer goes something like this: 'Aye, they'll be up soon, the fish', then darkly as an afterthought, 'If they're in the mood, that is.'

Although a ghillie can do a great many things, you must remember that he's not responsible for the weather or the height of the water. In other words, it's not his fault if you don't take home a salmon, and yes, I have met anglers who take it out on the ghillie on blank days. He's not a magician and if the fish aren't there, or they are there but they aren't taking, you can't really blame the poor old ghillie. If you get really tired and fed up you can ask him to fish your rod. Now, the purists will be enraged by such a suggestion, but as we already know, a beginner can learn an awful lot just by watching. Some ghillies I've seen have rather unorthodox ways of casting, but they nearly always catch a salmon, so who cares! And when they do catch a fish, you still get to keep it.

A witty ghillie will keep you amused for hours. Like the one who related the tale of the young man who came to fish with his new bride. Almost a fishing honeymoon, you might say, though probably more so for him than for her. Well, he duly fished and she duly watched, until at last he hooked a salmon and under the watchful gaze of his adoring young wife, he proudly pulled it into the shallows. At this point, though, she couldn't stand it any longer and she rushed down to the water, threw her arms around him, kissed him and accidentally stood on the line and pulled it clean out the fish's mouth. At this point in the tale the ghillie's voice became sombre. 'They're divorced now of course,' he said, 'though I'm not sure that was the main cause.'

But the entertainment's not all one-way and most appreciate being asked about their family and past jobs, as long as you're not too nosey. The river, you'll find, is a great leveller as there's really only one topic of conversation. A cat may look at a king when fishing, or a ghillie at a prince. There's the famous story of the man who was working with foreign royalty and was rowing him across the river in a small boat when the prince happened to hook a salmon. 'Keep your rod tip up, Your Highness', urged the ghillie, as the man struggled to keep his cool. 'That's good', soothed the ghillie, 'you're doing just fine. Yes, that's lovely, Your Highness. Now, wind him in slowly and remember to keep the tip up. Keep it up, that's right, Your Highness, that's just fine. Now don't let him get behind that rock...and keep the tip UP Your Highness! UP!

In the hut at Upper Dunkeld. Mike Bullough sporting neoprenes as usual!

UP! Oh, you great daft bugger... you've lost him!'

Now speaking to your betters like this runs the risk of being carted off to the Tower of London but the tale goes that our prince was so amused that he insisted on that ghillie always attending to him on future trips. He also tipped him royally, for although a ghillie is generally paid by whoever owns the beat, it's customary to give him something extra for his pains. It depends on where you're fishing as to the amount, so check with other fishers as to how much. We usually work on at least five pounds a day per fisher and double that if a salmon is caught.

Just how far the comradeship goes is up to both of you, but I've noticed that offers to stay and share lunch are usually gratefully received but politely declined, as most ghillies know what they like and what they don't. An ancient ghillie on the Tay who'd been a prisoner-of-war in Germany was reminiscing about his time in the camps. 'It wasn't that bad', he said, 'it was just the food we were given to eat. Pretty dull stuff it was too, like dry bread and boiled cabbage. Yes, terribly plain, so I pitied the fellows who'd been used to eating all that fancy food back home. I was all right though,' he continued. 'I'd been brought up in the Highlands and was used to simple things like salmon, grouse and venison.' Quite!

And if you've a ghillie on your beat, the chances are you'll also have a hut. This is literally what it sounds like, a small building rather like a garden shed by the side of the river. It may be bare and basic, but on cold, wet days, it becomes a haven, a place to eat in and shelter from the elements. Most huts I've seen are quite basic with just a rickety old wooden table and a bench or two, but others come with all mod cons like lighting and heating. Some are definitely over the top, like the one I heard of complete with telephone and fax, though I must say that these luxurious ones are the exception rather than the rule and anyway, what sort of angler wants a telephone? Surely part of the joy of fishing is to leave the office behind?!

But back to our hut. As a guest, you must treat it with respect and leave it tidy for the next lot. The ghillie will usually help, though some are more house-proud than others, like the legendary man from the Spey who used to lay his hut table like a five-star dining room, complete with polished glasses, cutlery, napkins and all!

Whatever it's like though, a hut is a wonderful way of making fishing a sociable occasion. Here, after the day's strenuous efforts, you and your party can unwind and tell huge lies about the ones that got away. Not all fishers drink, but those that do generally catch more fish in the hut than they ever do by the river. Some huts, of course, you enter at your own risk...

My father-in-law tells the story of how he was casting away on Deeside one summer's night when he was invited into a neighbouring hut by another fishing party. 'Well, there's no harm in that', he thought, 'just a quick drink to be sociable.' A quick drink indeed! He went in at ten o'clock and it was eight singing, drinking, storytelling hours later — six o'clock in the morning — when he finally emerged, bleary-eyed and well the worse for wear. A good night was had by all, I understand. The only one who didn't think it jolly was my mother-in-law, who'd been expecting him back for dinner at the hotel! Whether this is the legendary hut endearingly nicknamed 'The Drammerie' by visiting fishers, I don't know. All I do know is that huts in general are places where licensing hours don't apply, and those with a weak constitution perhaps shouldn't venture in.

It's on nights like this that tall tales are told. You've heard the old saying, 'How far an angler will stretch the truth depends on how far he can stretch his arms.' Like the fisher who was boasting about the size of his latest salmon, 'It must have been five feet at least,' he said proudly, after a few drinks. 'Aye', said the ghillie who was sitting listening, 'I've got a good story too to tell you. It's about those divers who have been searching the wreckage of a Spanish galleon off the Scottish coast. Well, do you know the latest. They got down to the seabed to find that everything was intact. Nothing had been touched. In fact it was so unspoiled that the ship's lantern was still burning. Imagine, still aflame after all these years and in all that water!'

'Nonsense,' said the fisher, 'that's ridiculous. The lantern still burning? I don't believe that at all!'

'Well I'll tell you what I'll do,' said the ghillie. 'You cut a couple of feet off your fish, and I'll blow out the lantern.'

Or the non-fisher who walks into a hut and finds all these noisy anglers boasting about salmon sizes, arms outstretched three, four, no five feet wide. And there in the corner is a quiet, little man with his hands just a foot apart. 'Well now,' said the visitor, 'you're a man who tells the truth. A salmon twelve inches long, that's more like it.'

'Oh no,' said the small fisher, 'that distance was the width between his eyes.'!

And then there are the ones that get away, and a ghillie on the River Almond in Perthshire who regularly helped them to. On desperate, fishless days, this man would stick his thermometer into the water and tell his fishers, 'Ye may as well stay in the hut, gentlemen. Ye'll have to bonk them over the heed if ye want to get them oot today!'

'Honestly, IT WAS!'

Some, though, aren't lost, even though they deserve to be. Sitting in a hut on the banks of the River Eden, our friend the late Michael Cartmell told how he once caught two magnificent salmon whilst fishing the River Derwent in West Cumbria. Laying them carefully in the back of his van, he set off proudly for home, but as he was driving along, the back door suddenly burst open and the fish slid out. It was only when he got back to the house that Michael realised what had happened, so he retraced his steps, although at this stage, he thought they must surely be lost forever. But, lo and behold, four miles back down the road, lying in the middle of the busy dual-carriageway were two large, silvery fish, still there and still intact, with cars and lorries swerving round them. A happy ending to what could have been a disaster!

Disasters are studiously avoided when talking about fishing, as are sensitive issues. They just aren't discussed. Like the day we were out with a man whose wife had just left him for another, a non-angler, of course, though I can't imagine why. The man was obviously suffering, though nobody referred to this private grief. One of our party sympathetically remarked, 'One doesn't want to spoil a chap's fishing by mentioning it.'

No earthquakes, no political rows, no scandal. In short, the only news an angler wants to hear when he's down at the river is about the latest feathered fly or lightweight line. And here we come full circle, if not with a fishing net, at least with the book.

From newscaster to fly-caster. Now there's a good title for a book or a headline for a story! When I was researching this book, I was told a story by the fisher and writer, Malcolm Greenhalgh. He was being filmed by a television crew, who arrived, set up their equipment and started shooting. Well, they worked away and Malcolm worked away, but half-an-hour into the proceedings, the lads appeared to be getting a bit restless. 'Right, you can catch a fish any time now', they shouted. Then, after another few minutes. 'Right, we're ready for a fish now!'

I know that this sort of thing happens because over the years I've been interviewed and photographed by magazines and national newspapers who like the idea of a well known woman fisher. So, they arrive, all of them jolly chaps, cameras at the ready, pens poised for the exclusive. Then it's, 'It would be nice to have a fish for this photograph', and when nothing transpires, 'You know, it really would be nice if you could catch a fish...!' Look, I know it would be nice if I caught a fish, in those conditions it would a damn miracle!

I did oblige once, though, and that was five minutes after a photographer from the *Daily Mirror* had given up and gone home! However, I rang him up to boast about my catch and, bless him, he did return, making the 200 mile round-journey once again to record the evidence, a 14-pound salmon!

Or even the 'F' factor, an unfortunate term I seemed to get stuck with during my brief time with GMTV. 'F' was for flirting, they said, for fanciability. But 'F' is also for other things; for family — most important of all — for the future, for friends and fly-fishing. I hope you think so too.

And here I had hoped to end the book, but it's a rather serious way to end what I hope's been an informative, but light-hearted look at fishing. And, apart from which, my father-in-law, Tommy has just come in with a poem which he says sums up the whole thing. 'I don't know why you've bothered to write all those chapters', he says. 'You could just have told them to read this! Now, this has everything that a beginner fishing for salmon needs to know.' Well, see what you think, if you can understand it, that is! Tight lines!

The Rules O' The Game

When you're fishing for salmon,	
That is wi' the flea*	fly
There's some things ye mauna*	must not
And some ye maun dee.*	must do
Be it cauld, weet or het,*	cold, wet or hot
Bright, lowering, or clear,	
Aye*, fish wi' the flea,	always
What ere ye mon* hear.	might
There are fleas o 'a' colours	
And ithers beside.	
But pey nae* attention,	pay no
Let size be your guide.	
Gin* he rises gey* and often,	Until, lively
But willna* tak hud,*	will not, hold
A smaller flea try,	
Then wait for the thud.	
When watters are big,	
Fish the tail o' the stream,	
Wi' a muckle* big flea	large
And some lead.	
It may spoil your casting	
And will glisten maybe,	
But the fish on the bottom	
Will hae something tae see.	
When salmon they tak,	
Wi a sworle on the tap,	
Dinna* strike like at troots,*	Don't, trout
Or your line will gang* slack.	go
But wait till he turns	
Has the hook i' his throat.	
A flick o' the tip,	
Is 'a' that is sought.	
But if its deep doon he taks,	
Wi' a thud that near shaks ye,	
He's hookit* already,	hooked
Nae more tae dae.	
But up wi' the pint*	tip
And put on the strain	
Get richt up ammenst* him,	amongst
He'll go like a train.	

Now counter each move,
Wi' just enough force.
And lead him tae safety,
Like driving a horse!
For he jump, drop the pint.
Let the line gang slack
And pray he is still there and
Soon will be back.
Then up pint again
And tak up the strain
And soon in your bag,
Yee'll be takin' him hame.
Through the day noo 'n* then,   *now and*
Take time tae sit doon.
Mak sure that your line knots
And hooks are a' soon.*   *sound*
Check the pint o' yore hook,
It should aye be richt sharp.
Keep a file in your bag,
It will pay for the work.
Ye think he's played oot
When he turns on his back.
But he's aye got anither
Trump caird in the pack
And just as ye slack line
And reach oot
Tae fit on the tailer
Or stick in the hook
He revives at yince,*   *once*
Wi' a dive and a splash
A flick o' his tail
And he's gane* in a flash   *gone*
Now if you pay attention
Tae all that I say
Sport will ensue,
Some time i' the day
But wait, haud* a minit,   *hold on*
Consider, think again.
Hae the salmon be telled
The RULES O' THE GAME?   *Anon*

Glossary

ANGLING CLUB	Fishing association. Make sure they've got some fly-fishing water!
BACKING	Thin, plaited nylon or heavy monofilament which goes onto the reel before the line. Your backing is the back-up to the line.
BACKING-UP METHOD	Where the fisher starts at the tail of the pool and works upstream. Used when the water is very still and you want to get more movement into your fly.
BARB	The jagged bit on the hook of the fly.
BEAT	A fishing river is divided into stretches of waters called beats. A beat varies in length up to several miles long.
BUTT	The handle, often made of cork, on your fly rod.
CAST or LEADER	The nylon, the link between line and fly.
CASTING	The craft of using your rod to throw your line, leader and fly across the water and over the fish.
CLOSE SEASON	The period of time when rivers are not fished, to allow spawning to take place.
COCK	A male salmon.
COVER WATER	To fish over water thoroughly.
DOUBLE	Fly with two-pronged hook.
DRAM	Gaelic for a large tot of whisky. Scotland has around 115 distilleries so there's no excuse!
DROPPER	The second fly attached from the centre of your leader. In theory, it gives two chances of a fish, or even two fish!
ELVIN	The first stage after the egg in the life cycle of the salmon.

FERULES	The joints of a rod. The rod ferules slot together to form the long rod.
FIGURE OF EIGHT KNOT	Knot used to join line to leader.
FLY	Feathered hook to attract the fish.
FLY BOX	A box to keep your flies in.
FLY-TYING	The art of making a fly. Try making you own!
FLY- HOLDER	The small circle of wire above the rod butt to which the fly is attached to stop it flailing about in the wind when not fishing.
FLOATING LINE	Line that floats on the water surface. Used more often in summer when levels are lower.and water temperatures higher
FOUL HOOK	To hook a fish somewhere other than in its mouth. Foul-hooked fish must be returned to the water.
FRY	The tiny fish that emerges from the salmon egg.
GAFF	Metal hook used to land a fish. Not widely used these days.
GHILLIE	Sportsman's attendant in the Highlands, the helper. Invaluable, entertaining, delightful!
GREASING	To grease a knot is to wet it, spit is fine, before you pull it tight. Paradoxically, it stops it from slipping loose again.
GRILSE	A young salmon which has returned to spawn after just one sea winter. Delicious to eat!
HALF-BLOOD KNOT	Common knot to join fly to leader.
HANDLINING	To slowly pull in line as it fishes round in the water. To inject movement into the fly and make it seem more lifelike to the fish.
HEN	A female salmon.
HOOK	Either single, double or treble.
HUT	Often at the side of the beat. Like a garden hut, useful to eat lunch in or shelter in if the weather is really bad.
KELT	A salmon that has spawned and is heading back down river to the sea. Eel-like, kelts are inedible and if caught, should be

put back.

LAND A FISH	To bring him to the bank or shore or into the net.
LEADER	Your nylon, the link between line and fly. (See also CAST)
LIE	Good place to fish over, as salmon like to find a good lie in the river.
LIFE JACKET	Possible life saver. Wear a proper angling one if the water looks dodgy!
LINE	Your line is the next thing on your reel after the backing and it's the line that takes leader and fly out across the water.
MITTENS	Gloves cut off at the joints, useful to feel the line, yet still keep hands warm.
NET	For salmon. A large, unwieldy object, useful for getting the fish from the water to the bank!
NYLON	The link between line and fly, often known as a cast or leader.
OVERHEAD CAST	The standard cast when fly-fishing. Take the rod back and then arc it forward, allowing the line to come shooting out down the rod.
PARR	A young salmon, a little fish of between three and five inches.
PERMIT	Either written or verbal, everyone needs a permit to fish.
PLAY A FISH	The term given to the battle between the angler and the fish once he's on the hook. It means giving him line when he tries to run and reeling him in when he tires.
POACHING	Definitely not allowed! Fishing without permission, or using illegal methods.
POOL	The river is divided into pools and fish rest in pools before heading upstream again. A good place to fish over.
PRIEST	The heavy, blunt instrument like a small truncheon used to kill the fish with when you catch it.
PULL	When the fish takes your fly and then spits it out, you have "had a pull".. Still, there's some momentary excitement and

at least you know there's something in the river!

REEL — The contraption your backing and line goes onto and which sits on the rod. You wind in your reel to pull in a fish.

REEL SEAT — Where your reel sits when it's attached to the rod.

RINGS — The wire guides on the rod through which the line is threaded.

ROD — The long, sticklike instrument used to throw your line across the water. Also, my husband's name!

ROD LICENCE — Needed in England, Wales and Northern Ireland, though not in Scotland.

RUN — Salmon are on a run when returning up-river to spawn.

SHOOT LINE — To use your rod to send line shooting through the rings on the rod and across the water.

SINKING LINE — Line that sinks in the water to take the fly down to the fish. Used often in cold weather and when levels are high.

SLEEVE — The cover for your rod, made of fabric, plastic or metal. Antique ones are made of leather.

SPEY CAST — Forward, rather than backward cast. Useful in the wind or where there are bushes or trees behind you.

STRIKE — To strike. What you must do when you think there's a fish on the end of your line, bring the rod tip up smoothly, to try to hook the fish securely.

TACKLE — Your fishing equipment.

TACKLE SHOP — Where you buy your fishing equipment.

TACKLE BAG — What you put your tackle in, eg reel, flies, etc.

TAILER — Metal instrument used to land a fish by looping it around its tail.

TENANT — The person who rents the fishing.

TIMESHARE — Where you buy fishing for a week or two per year, for a fixed term of several years or in perpetuity.

TIP RING	The final wire eye on the tip of your rod.
TO MEND LINE	To create an upstream or downstream curve in the line to hold back or accelerate the passage of the line and thus the fly. Do this by swinging the rod tip and the line should follow.
TOUCH A FISH	When a fish nibbles at your fly, you have touched a fish.
TREBLE	Fly with three-pronged hook.
TUBE FLY	Fly where the body comes separate from the hook. Useful if you break a barb, you just replace the hook, not the whole thing.
WADDINGTON	A type of fly.
WADERS	Extended wellies. Essential for staying dry when wading. Thigh waders come to the thigh, chest waders to the chest.
WADING STICK	Stick made out of wood or metal, weighted at the end, to help you move more steadily in the water.
WIND KNOTS	Tiny knots that appear in the nylon as it flails about in the wind and snap it when a fish is hooked. A common complaint for the beginner!